W9-BVJ-043

Women of Achievement

Ruth Bader Ginsburg

Women of Achievement

Abigail Adams
Susan B. Anthony
Tyra Banks
Clara Barton
Hillary Rodham Clinton
Marie Curie
Ellen DeGeneres
Diana, Princess of Wales
Tina Fey
Ruth Bader Ginsburg
Joan of Arc
Helen Keller
Madonna
Michelle Obama
Sandra Day O'Connor
Georgia O'Keeffe
Nancy Pelosi
Rachael Ray
Anita Roddick
Eleanor Roosevelt
Martha Stewart
Barbara Walters
Venus and Serena Williams

Women of Achievement

Ruth Bader Ginsburg

U.S. SUPREME COURT JUSTICE

Paul McCaffrey

CHELSEA HOUSE
PUBLISHERS
An imprint of Infobase Publishing

RUTH BADER GINSBURG

Chelsea House
An imprint of Infobase Publishing
132 West 31st Street
New York, NY 10001

Library of Congress Cataloging-in-Publication Data
McCaffrey, Paul, 1977–
 Ruth Bader Ginsburg : U.S. Supreme Court justice / by Paul McCaffrey.
 p. cm. — (Women of achievement)
 Includes bibliographical references and index.
 ISBN 978-1-60413-687-6 (hardcover)
 1. Ginsburg, Ruth Bader. 2. Judges—United States—Biography. 3. United States. Supreme Court—Biography. [1. Women—Legal status, laws, etc.—United States.] I. Title. II. Series.

 KF8745.G56M33 2010
 347.73'2634—dc22
 [B]
                          2009051337

Chelsea House books are available at special discounts when purchased in bulk quantities for businesses, associations, institutions, or sales promotions. Please call our Special Sales Department in New York at (212) 967-8800 or (800) 322-8755.

You can find Chelsea House on the World Wide Web at http://www.chelseahouse.com

Text design by Erik Lindstrom
Cover design by Ben Peterson
Composition by EJB Publishing Services
Cover printed by Bang Printing, Brainerd, Minn.
Book printed and bound by Bang Printing, Brainerd, Minn.
Date printed: August 2010
Printed in the United States of America
10 9 8 7 6 5 4 3 2 1

This book is printed on acid-free paper.

All links and Web addresses were checked and verified to be correct at the time of publication. Because of the dynamic nature of the Web, some addresses and links may have changed since publication and may no longer be valid.

CONTENTS

An Announcement in the Rose Garden

After a three-month search for a candidate to fill the seat of the retiring Byron R. White, President Bill Clinton finally settled on his nominee to serve as the one hundred-seventh justice of the United States Supreme Court. He made his announcement at a sunny press conference in the Rose Garden of the White House on June 14, 1993. With the nominee's extended family in attendance, before members of the media, and with numerous government officials and other notables looking on, President Clinton introduced his choice, Ruth Bader Ginsburg, the second woman ever nominated to the country's highest court.

For those unfamiliar with Ginsburg's many achievements, the president filled them in. Ginsburg had served for 13 years on the U.S. Court of Appeals for the District of

Columbia, what many viewed as the second most influential court in the land. "[In] her years on the bench," the president remarked, "she has genuinely distinguished herself as one of our nation's best judges: progressive in outlook, wise in judgment, balanced and fair in her opinions."[1] Before her service on the Court of Appeals, Ginsburg taught as a full professor at Columbia University School of Law and Rutgers University School of Law. Outside of the academy, she worked for the Women's Rights Project (WRP), a part of the American Civil Liberties Union (ACLU). The WRP is a legendary effort to establish the legal framework of gender equality and women's rights in U.S. courts. In the process, the president noted, "She has compiled a truly historic record of achievement in the finest traditions of American law and citizenship."[2] Ginsburg's contributions toward women's equality were influenced in no small way by the second-class treatment she had received throughout her career—in college, law school, and the professional world. In his speech, with Ginsburg by his side, Clinton recognized her "pioneering work on behalf of the women of this country," noting that:

> Having experienced discrimination, she devoted the next 20 years of her career to fighting it and making this country a better place for our wives, our mothers, our sisters and our daughters. She argued and won many of the women's rights cases before the Supreme Court in the 1970s. Many admirers of her work say she is to the women's movement what former Supreme Court Justice Thurgood Marshall was to the movement for the rights of African Americans.[3]

His decision, Clinton informed his audience, was not one made lightly. "Article 2, Section 2 of the United States

Constitution empowers the President to select a nominee to fill a vacancy on the Supreme Court of the United States," he stated. "This responsibility is one of the most significant duties assigned to the President."[4] Whoever is selected and subsequently confirmed is appointed for life. Once on the Supreme Court, the justice will be one of nine who together have the final say on all constitutional matters. Each Supreme Court justice, the president intoned, "decides the most significant questions of our time and shapes the continuing contours of our liberty." Consequently, he remarked, "I know well how the Supreme Court affects the lives of all Americans personally and deeply."[5] Offering the highest compliment to his nominee, Clinton commented, "If, as I believe, the measure of a person's values can best be measured by examining the life the person lives, then Judge Ginsburg's values are the very ones that represent the best in America."[6]

Once the president finished, Ginsburg, a small 60-year-old grandmother, her hair pulled back into a neat bun, took to the podium. With a gorgeous sun shining down and unable to hide the smile peeking out from the corners of her mouth, Ginsburg thanked all those in attendance. To Clinton, she said, "Mr. President, I am grateful beyond measure for the confidence you have placed in me, and I will strive with all that I have to live up to your expectations in making this appointment." She vowed to work "to the best of my ability for the advancement of the law in the service of society."[7]

Ginsburg next introduced her family to the assembled crowd:

I have been aided by my life's partner, Martin D. Ginsburg, who has been since our teenage years my best friend and biggest booster; by my mother-in-law, Evelyn Ginsburg, the most supportive parent a

President Bill Clinton and his nominee for the U.S. Supreme Court, Ruth Bader Ginsburg, field questions from reporters during a news conference at the White House in Washington D.C., on June 14, 1993.

person could have; and by a daughter and son with the taste to appreciate that Daddy cooks ever so much better than Mommy—and so phased me out of the kitchen at a relatively early age.[8]

Ginsburg, however, saved her most heartfelt words for someone not in attendance, someone who had been gone for more than 40 years: her mother. At every major moment of Ginsburg's life—graduations, marriage, Supreme Court appearances, her swearing-in ceremony as a judge on the court of appeals—she had made a habit of wearing jewelry that belonged to her deceased mother. This day was no different.

"I have a last thank-you," she stated, her eyes watering behind her glasses.

> It is to my mother, Celia Amster Bader, the bravest and strongest person I have known, who was taken from me much too soon. I pray that I may be all that she would have been had she lived in an age when women could aspire and achieve and daughters are cherished as much as sons.[9]

The touching tribute brought tears to the president's eyes. As he and Ginsburg took questions from the press, he continued to heap on the praise. For all the uncertainty that had surrounded Clinton's search, few could quibble with his final choice: in Ginsburg, he had found precisely the person he was looking for.

Ginsburg's introduction as the president's nominee had come off perfectly. The next step in her bid for the Supreme Court, however, would take her to the halls of Congress and the U.S. Senate, where she would appear before the Senate Judiciary Committee. They would question her views and analyze her earlier court decisions. Some of the questions she would have to answer were likely to be about such hot-button issues as race and abortion. It was not going to be an easy task. But anyone familiar with Ginsburg's biography would not have bet against her. She had long since proved that there was no challenge to which she could not rise.

Tragedy and Achievement: The Early Years

Ruth Bader Ginsburg's 60-year journey to the Rose Garden on that sunny day in 1993 had not been an easy one. It was marked at nearly every step by discrimination, heartbreaking tragedy, and tragedy narrowly avoided. Yet through perseverance, talent, and unflagging purpose, Ginsburg overcame these obstacles.

Like countless American success stories, that of the one hundred-seventh justice of the U.S. Supreme Court began in a diverse immigrant community in New York City. Ruth Bader Ginsburg was born Joan Ruth Bader on March 15, 1933, in the borough of Brooklyn, the second daughter of Nathan Bader and the former Celia Amster. Nathan came to the United States from Russia with his parents at the age of 13. Celia was a native-born American, her parents having arrived in the United States from a town near Kraków, Poland, several months before her birth. Of the Jewish faith, both the Amsters and Baders fled Eastern Europe to escape the widespread and often violent anti-Semitism of their homelands and to pursue the economic opportunity promised by the American dream.

After marrying, Nathan and Celia resided on the first floor of a small two-story building in the Flatbush neighborhood of Brooklyn. Nathan owned and operated a small clothing shop, making coats, hats, and other garments, and he later worked for a men's clothing store. Celia helped her husband run his business but spent most of her time at home, keeping house and caring for her children. In the 1930s, Flatbush was filled with Irish, Italian, and Jewish families, many of them immigrants, who struggled to overcome the widespread poverty and joblessness of the Great Depression and build a better life for themselves.

Like many women of her day, Celia did not pursue an advanced education, despite her considerable intellect. Remarkably gifted, she graduated from high school at the age of 15, but rather than continue her studies, she instead went to work, earning money to help send her older brother, Solomon, to college. Though she was never able to continue her schooling, Celia maintained a love of reading throughout her life, a passion she passed on to Ruth. She also developed a strong commitment to women's education and vowed that her daughter would not miss out on opportunities as she had. In keeping with this wish, soon after Ruth was born, Celia began saving money to send her to college.

A SISTER LOST

Ruth's early life was touched by tragedy: When she was still a toddler, her older sister, Marilyn, then eight years old, was stricken with meningitis, a disease that attacks the brain and spinal cord. Then, as now, meningitis is a deadly illness, and Marilyn soon passed away. Though Ruth has little memory of her older sister, her loss was keenly felt and drew the Baders, already a tight-knit family, even closer together.

For the first four years of Ruth's life, the Baders shared their home with relatives. In an unusual twist of fate, Celia's sister had married Nathan's brother, blurring the line between sister and sister-in-law and brother and brother-in-law. The two couples shared living expenses and raised their children together. Because of this, Ruth was especially close with her cousin Richard. Born three

IN HER OWN WORDS

In her testimony before the Senate during her confirmation hearings, Ruth Bader Ginsburg recalled:

> I am . . . a first-generation American on my father's side, barely second-generation on my mother's. Neither of my parents had the means to attend college, but both taught me to love learning, to care about people, and to work hard for whatever I wanted or believed in. Their parents had the foresight to leave the old country, when Jewish ancestry and faith meant exposure to pogroms and deni-gration of one's human worth.*

* U.S. Congress. Senate Committee on the Judiciary. *Nomination of Ruth Ginsburg to be Associate Justice of the Supreme Court of the United States.* Hearings. 103rd Cong., 1st sess., July 20–23, 1993, p. 49.

months apart, the two children were constant companions, though their relationship was not without conflict. In fact, Marilyn dubbed Ruth "Kiki" after seeing her kick Richard. (The nickname stuck, and many of her childhood companions still refer to her by it.) Ruth was called "Ruth" rather than "Joan" after she started kindergarten; when registering Ruth for school, Celia found that there were already a couple of Joan Ruths in the class, so she signed up her daughter as Ruth Joan Bader.

Though the two Bader-Amster families eventually moved into separate residences, they stayed in the same neighborhood—as did many other members of their extended family—and continued to play important roles in one another's lives.

A LOVE OF READING

Among Ruth's fondest recollections of her childhood was the time she spent reading with her mother. Celia would take her to their local library branch, which was near a Chinese food restaurant, causing Ruth to associate "the aroma of Chinese food with the pleasures of reading."[1] Or she would bring Ruth to the main branch of the Brooklyn Public Library at Grand Army Plaza, where they would immerse themselves in stacks of books. In her youth, Ruth enjoyed reading Greek and Roman mythology and children's favorites such as *Winnie-the-Pooh* by A.A. Milne and *The Secret Garden* by Frances Hodgson Burnett. Ruth had a special fondness for mysteries featuring the enterprising young female detective Nancy Drew, "because she was smarter than her boyfriend,"[2] but also because "she was adventuresome, daring, and her boyfriend was a much more passive type than she was."[3]

In fact, many of Ruth's early role models, both real and fictional, were women who, like Nancy Drew, succeeded in fields that were normally the preserve of men. In particular,

The main branch of the Brooklyn Public Library at dusk. As a child, Ruth Bader Ginsburg often went to this library with her mother. Here, a love of reading and learning was passed from mother to child.

she found inspiration in stories about Pallas Athena, the Greek goddess of wisdom and the arts, as well as in the accomplishments of the American aviator Amelia Earhart, who with her daring successes as both a pilot and business-woman set an impressive example to millions of women of Ruth's era.

Ruth attended grammar school at PS 238 in Brooklyn, where her considerable talents were hard to overlook. A gifted student, Ruth excelled in the classroom, but she also was popular with her peers, and her many extracur-ricular activities show her to have been exceptionally well rounded. She was a member of the student orchestra, acted in school plays, and participated in school sports. When she was 12 or 13, she authored an editorial for PS 238's mimeographed newspaper, the *Highway Herald*. Titled "Landmarks of Constitutional Freedom," the piece described how several famous legal documents—among them the Ten Commandments; the Magna Carta, which established certain rights for the English nobility in 1215; and the Declaration of Independence—helped shape modern concepts like human rights and constitutional government. Even at this early age, Ruth displayed the makings of a first-rate legal mind. Outside of school, she excelled in other areas, receiving her confirmation, with high honors, at the East Midwood Jewish Center. Ruth graduated from PS 238 on June 24, 1946, one of two co-valedictorians. She also received a scholarship for her stellar academic record and service to the school.

After completing her primary education, Ruth went on to James Madison High School in Brooklyn, one of the top high schools in New York City. Even in an institution with more than its share of gifted students, she managed to stand out. Ann Burkhardt Kittner, a friend and fellow student, recalled, "She had piercing blue eyes and a certain magnetism that drew people to her."[4] As at PS 238, Ruth succeeded brilliantly in her classes and was equally committed to extracurricular pursuits. She was an editor of the school newspaper and served in the Go-Getters Club, a pep group that wore black satin jackets, sold tickets to school football games, and rallied the student body for big events. Indeed, while twirling a baton during a Madison football game against Lincoln High, Ruth managed to chip a tooth. She also played cello in the school orchestra, ran for student government, worked on the high school yearbook, and belonged to the Arista honors society. Though extremely driven, Ruth did not go out of her way to seek attention and was exceptionally modest. Her friend Harryette Gordon Hessel remembered, "Ruth wouldn't speak unless she had something to say. She was always thinking. You might not even have realized she was listening until suddenly she'd say what was on her mind."[5]

Ruth Bader Ginsburg grew up in a vibrant, hardscrabble Brooklyn, New York, where hardworking immigrant families were as common as the borough's trolley cars. Though now defunct, the Brooklyn trolleys have one enduring legacy—the Los Angeles Dodgers baseball team, originally from Brooklyn, was once known as the Trolley Dodgers.

During the summers, Ruth would leave the sweltering streets of Brooklyn for upstate New York's Adirondack Mountains, where she attended Camp Che-Na-Wah, an all-girls Jewish summer camp run by her uncle and aunt, Sol ("Chuck") and Cornelia Amster. At Camp Che-Na-Wah, located on Lake Balfour, Ruth and her fellow campers could take in the natural beauty of the surrounding environment and participate in athletics, arts and crafts, and other activities. Ruth particularly enjoyed horseback riding and eventually served as a camp counselor.

DID YOU KNOW?

A public high school located on Bedford Avenue in the Midwood neighborhood of Brooklyn, James Madison High School opened in 1925. In the 80-plus years since, to say the school's alumni have done their alma mater proud would be a vast understatement. Ruth Bader Ginsburg (Class of 1950) is just one of the many Madison graduates to have left their mark on the world. Named after the fourth president of the United States, a man who has been dubbed the "Father of the Constitution," James Madison High School has perhaps not surprisingly produced more than its share of politicians, including Charles Schumer (Class of 1967), who represents New York in the United States Senate; Bernard Sanders (Class of 1959), a senator from Vermont; and Norman Coleman (Class of 1966), who served one term in the Senate for Minnesota. The school also has racked up Nobel Prize winners: Stanley Cohen (Class of 1939) earned the honor in the field of medicine, Martin Perl (Class of 1941) in physics, and both Robert Solow (Class of 1940) and Gary Becker (Class of 1948) in economics. Nor is Ruth Bader Ginsburg the only famous judge to have come out of James Madison: television's Judge Judy, Judith Sheindlin, is an alumna. In the field of entertainment, the award-winning actor Martin Landau is a former student at Madison, as are comedians Andrew Dice Clay and Chris Rock, who spent some of his high school days there but transferred out before graduating. Among the school's athletes are Frank Torre, a former major league baseball player and brother of Los Angeles Dodgers' manager Joe Torre, and the Olympic athlete and sports broadcaster Marty Glickman.

A TERRIBLE SECRET

Blessed with a wide circle of friends and excelling both in and outside the classroom, Ruth Bader appeared to be navigating her high school years quite well. Few of her friends, however, knew the terrible burden she was carrying. When Ruth was only a freshman, her mother was diagnosed with cervical cancer. A long and terrible battle with the disease followed as Celia's condition seemed to grow worse with each passing day. After completing her activity-filled days at school, Ruth would head home and sit by her ailing mother's bedside. Adding to the family's troubles, with Celia too ill to help Nathan manage his business, the Baders' financial predicament worsened. Finally, four years after her initial diagnosis and on the eve of Ruth's high school graduation, Celia Amster Bader, with her family by her side, passed away at the age of 47.

Rather than attend her high school graduation, Ruth instead went to bury her mother. Her teachers delivered the many awards and accolades she had earned during her four years at James Madison personally to her house. These honors included the Parents' Association Award for Citizenship, an English Scholarship Medal, and a place in the Round Table Forum of Honor.

Throughout her daughter's life, Celia Bader had scrimped and saved so that Ruth would not miss out on the chance to go to college like she had. Yet the $5,000 she managed to accumulate to finance her daughter's education would hardly be needed for tuition. Having graduated sixth in a class of 700, Ruth earned a New York state scholarship and admission to the Ivy League. In the fall of 1950, Ruth Bader left Brooklyn for upstate New York, where she would attend Cornell University. The money her mother had saved to send her to school was instead given to her father to help his business.

A Legal Mind
Takes Shape

In the fall of 1950, Ruth Bader arrived at Cornell University in Ithaca, New York, still stricken with grief over her mother's death. Even so, as at James Madison, she immediately began to establish a record of achievement in academics and extracurricular activities. She joined Alpha Epsilon Phi, one of only two Jewish sororities at Cornell at the time, as well as the Women's Self Governance Association. Alpha Epsilon Phi sponsored dances and teas and otherwise provided a social support network for Ruth as she sought a place for herself at Cornell.

Majoring in government, Ruth became a protégé of Professor Robert E. Cushman, who taught constitutional law. Ruth served as Cushman's research assistant and was deeply inspired by his example. In many ways,

Cushman helped persuade her to become a lawyer. She later wrote:

> At Cornell, where I was an undergraduate, I was influenced particularly by . . . Professor Robert Cushman. I studied with him and worked as his research assistant. That was in the mid-1950s, an interesting time, the heyday of McCarthyism. Cushman was a defender of our deep-seated national values—freedom of thought, speech and press. He wasn't outspoken about it. He was a very gentle man. His own credentials were impeccable. But he could not tolerate threats to our American way, whether from the left or from the right.[1]

Indeed, she has described the McCarthy era as

> a time when courageous lawyers were using their legal training in support of the right to think and speak freely. That a lawyer could do something that was personally satisfying and at the same time work to preserve the values that have made this country great was an exciting prospect for me.[2]

Cushman also helped shape Ruth's writing style, showing her that clear, direct language was essential for successful legal writing. Another professor, the Russian émigré Vladimir Nabokov, particularly influenced Ruth's writing. A towering figure in post–World War II literature, Nabokov is most remembered for his novel *Lolita*. Ruth wrote of Nabokov: "He loved words, the sound of words. . . . Even when I write an opinion, I will often read a sentence aloud and [ask,] 'Can I say this in fewer words—can I write it so the meaning will come across with greater clarity?'"[3]

The Russian émigré writer Vladimir Nabokov, author of *Lolita* and many other novels, was one of Ruth Bader Ginsburg's professors at Cornell. He would help her develop the clear writing style that has been a hallmark of her legal writing.

"THE DARK AGES"

Despite having such great professors, for Ruth life at Cornell was far from perfect. Especially troubling was the gender gap. Expectations for men and women were vastly different. On the athletic fields, women were required to wear raincoats over their uniforms. While men did not have a nightly curfew, women had to be back in their dormitories by a certain hour. Such rules, with their obvious double standards for men and women, were just one aspect of something larger and more troubling: the overall culture at Cornell did not encourage academic achievement by women. "There was a problem with Cornell in the '50s," Ginsburg recollected. "The most important degree for you to get was Mrs., and it didn't do to be seen reading and studying. . . . I knew some pretty obscure libraries on the Cornell campus." The more important thing, Ruth remembered, "was to be a party girl. It's long gone, but it was the tone of the '50s."[4] Even in the classroom, women were not always given their due. The assumption hanging over every female student was that they would not continue their education or pursue a career after they obtained their diplomas. While the men went on to graduate school or to work, the women, most believed, would go on to marry and have children. Consequently, students and teachers, male and female alike, saw the education of women as of slightly less importance.

This massive gulf in expectations was not something women at the time questioned. Feminism and equal rights were barely a whisper on campus. "I did not think of myself as a feminist in the 1950s," Ginsburg later remarked. "The subject never even came up in my conversations with classmates or teachers."[5] As Alice Freed, a friend of Ruth's, remembered, "We went to school in the dark ages. In our day, we accepted it."[6]

Students on campus of Cornell University in Ithaca, New York, in 1950, the year the future Supreme Court justice began her freshman year. While there, she met her future husband, Martin Ginsburg.

HER FUTURE HUSBAND

During her freshman year, Ruth met a man whose convictions were vastly different from the then-prevailing view of male-female relations. Raised on Long Island, New York, in a well-to-do family, Martin David Ginsburg did not come across as an especially serious student—or, for that matter, a logical match for the quiet and disciplined Ruth. He had given up his premedical major for chemistry in order to focus on his intercollegiate golfing. One of the few students on campus with a car—a gray Chevrolet—Martin met Ruth one night at her dormitory after he drove a friend there to pick up a date who lived next door to Ruth. Martin and Ruth did not fall in love immediately. "Ruth is a very quiet person," Martin would recollect. "Our first date was a pleasant but undistinguished evening."[7] They continued to see each other, Martin's outgoing personality melding nicely with Ruth's shy, studious demeanor—a classic case of opposites attracting. "We are not tremendously similar," Martin commented.

> I got the lowest passing grades in my class while she was the valedictorian of hers. I'm more talkative, but Ruth only speaks when she has something to say. That has never inhibited me. I like commercial subjects, and my wife has the "disadvantage" of doing well at everything.[8]

As their relationship blossomed, Ruth and Martin started to compete with each other, taking the same courses to see who could score higher. Most of the time, Ruth would win. Ruth later described Martin as "the only boy I knew who cared that I had a brain."[9] For his part, Martin found Ruth different from all the other women at Cornell, who all seemed to him to embrace the gender mentality that existed in the 1950s. He remarked: "Only about one in five students admitted [to Cornell] were women, so of course the women tended to be smarter. Still, in the main, these women had little interest in doing things. I never understood why that ought to be."[10]

In 1953, during Ruth's junior year, she and Martin became engaged. That same year, Martin graduated and went on to law school at Harvard University while Ruth remained at Cornell to complete her senior year. Throughout her time at Cornell, Ruth had contemplated a career in law. Though inspired by Professor Cushman, Ruth felt as though she lacked the necessary talent. Despite her doubts, she applied and was accepted to Harvard Law School. Harvard also offered her a scholarship.

GRADUATION AND MARRIAGE

In June 1954, Ruth Bader graduated from Cornell's College of Arts and Sciences. Having served as class marshal throughout her senior year, she stood at the head of her class in the graduation line. In addition to her Bachelor of Arts degree, she earned high honors in government and distinction in all subjects. She was likewise named to two honors societies, Phi Kappa Phi and Phi Beta Kappa. Soon after her graduation, on June 23, 1954, Ruth Bader and Martin Ginsburg were married in a small ceremony at the Ginsburg home in Rockville Center, New York.

Ginsburg's decision to continue her education at law school was not an easy one. Despite her impressive academic achievements, she still questioned her ability to succeed as a lawyer. There were other forces at work as well. Prospects for female attorneys in the 1950s were not especially bright. With not much money to leave Ruth and doubtful of a Jewish woman's chances in the legal field, her father felt she could best secure her future by becoming a teacher. Further complicating her decision was the fact that it would have to be postponed: Martin was drafted into the army, forcing him to put his own legal education on hold and take up a posting as an artillery officer at Fort Sill, Oklahoma. Before reporting for duty, however, Martin was granted a brief deferment, and the newlyweds spent a lengthy honeymoon traveling throughout Europe, with stops in Great Britain, Italy, France, and Switzerland.

GENDER DISCRIMINATION IN THE WORKPLACE

Following their honeymoon, the couple moved to Oklahoma. As Martin carried out his military duty, Ruth worked as a clerk typist at the local Social Security office in Lawton, Oklahoma. When hired, she received the government pay grade rating of GS-5. Given her record at college, the job did not make full use of her talents. Nevertheless, Ginsburg enjoyed helping people, particularly older Native Americans who were being denied their Social Security benefits because they lacked birth certificates. Using the dates from their driver's licenses or other forms of identification, Ginsburg made sure they received their full allotments.

Unfortunately, Ginsburg's tenure at the Social Security office was marred by discrimination. After discovering that she was pregnant, she made the mistake of telling her supervisors. Subsequently, she was demoted from the GS-5 pay grade down to a GS-2, which meant a substantial cut in her wages, and a trip she was scheduled to take to a training seminar in Baltimore, Maryland, was canceled. Sadly, this sort of treatment was not unusual for the time. Pregnant women were often viewed as risky propositions in the workplace. Many times it was assumed that they would need more rest and thus would not be as productive. Moreover, the social conventions of the time held that once a woman became a mother, she was expected to stay at home and raise her family. Consequently, in many respects a pregnancy was viewed as the equivalent of giving nine months' notice. Rather than fight this unfair treatment, Ginsburg, like most women of her day, accepted her fate without protest. The experience, however, shaped her outlook on the gender divide and later would inspire her to fight similar forms of discrimination as an attorney.

MOTHERHOOD

On July 21, 1955, Ruth Bader Ginsburg gave birth to a daughter, Jane Carol Ginsburg, in Freeport, New York, on Long Island. The couple had opted for a hospital they were familiar with rather than the military hospital at Fort Sill. For the next year, Ruth was a stay-at-home mother, caring for her daughter while Martin completed his military duty. That year was the only time as a parent that she did not work outside the home. For the 1950s, the Ginsburgs ran an unconventional household, with both husband and wife sharing duties normally reserved for the woman. The couple discovered early in their marriage that Martin was the better chef. Indeed, the first meal she ever prepared for him—a tuna casserole—was, Martin later recalled, "as close to inedible as food could be."[11]

FINDING A WAY

As Martin completed his service in the army, Ruth reapplied to Harvard Law School and was again accepted. After Martin was discharged in 1956, the young family moved back east to Cambridge, Massachusetts, so that both mother and father could take up their studies at Harvard.

Uneasy about the enormous responsibilities of marriage, motherhood, and Harvard, Ginsburg continued to wrestle with doubts about law school. Could she still care for her husband and their infant daughter while a full-time student? Even if she managed to graduate, would her status as a Jewish mother keep law firms from offering her a job?

Being a mother certainly had not helped her at the Social Security office. As always, Martin supported her fully, encouraging her to take on the challenge, knowing that she was more than up to it. But with so many doubts, not to mention her own father's hesitations, Ginsburg turned to her in-laws for advice.

What Morris Ginsburg, Martin's father, lacked in formal education, he made up for in judgment and intuition. Though he never completed high school, he managed to build a successful career as a businessman. Evelyn, Martin's mother, though well educated, chose to stay at home after marrying in order to raise her family. Having lost her own mother at an early age, Ruth often looked to Evelyn Ginsburg for advice and support. On the question of becoming an attorney, Morris Ginsburg provided his daughter-in-law with the wisdom that sealed her fate. He acknowledged that nobody would be disappointed if she opted against going to school, but that, as Ruth recollected, "if I really wanted to be a lawyer, having a baby wouldn't stand in my way. I realized he was absolutely right, and I think he gave me sound advice for most things in life. If you want to do something badly enough, you find a way. Somehow you manage."[12] So that's what the Ginsburgs did. They managed.

First they found an elderly sitter for Jane and arranged their school schedules so that one of them would always be home by four in the afternoon to relieve her. They split up the household duties between them to allow each of them the time they needed in the law library. In addition to taking care of the cooking, Martin also stayed up caring for Jane when she woke during the night, since he found it easier to fall back to sleep than Ruth did. She later confessed that without Martin's willingness to shoulder much of the burden of caring for Jane and their home, she very well could have dropped out of law school. "What Martin did went far beyond support," Ginsburg observed. "He believed in me more than I believed in myself."[13]

As for her own motivation for becoming a lawyer, Ginsburg admitted it was not entirely altruistic. "I became a lawyer for personal, selfish reasons. I thought I could do a lawyer's job better than any other. I have no talent in the arts but I do write fairly well and I analyze problems clearly."[14]

HARVARD LAW SCHOOL

Whatever her talents, Ginsburg found the challenge at Harvard Law School not merely an academic one. As at Cornell and the Social Security office in Oklahoma, the gender divide continued to be a difficult obstacle to over-come. In a class of about 500 students, there were only nine women, none of whom were made to feel entirely welcome. Early on, Ginsburg and her female classmates were invited to a dinner at the home of Erwin Griswold, a dean of the law school, where he rather bluntly asked them to justify taking up a seat in the law school that otherwise would have gone to a man. To avoid offending the dean, Ginsburg answered that studying law would help her grasp her husband's work and maybe allow her to find a part-time legal job.

Sadly, this was not the only example of blatant gender bias that Ginsburg and the other women would encounter at Harvard. In the law school dormitories, no rooms were reserved for women. As she recalled, "Women were not admitted to the Harvard Faculty Club dining tables. One could invite one's father but not one's wife or mother to the [*Harvard*] *Law Review* banquet."[15] The periodicals room at Harvard's Lamont Library was not open to women. This caused Ginsburg some difficulty one night when she needed to confirm a reference there. The guard would not allow her to enter and refused to bring the journal in question to her at the door. Finally, she had to find a male student to go in and obtain the source for her. With so few women at the law school, the few in attendance always stuck out. "If you were one of two women in a section," Ginsburg explained, "you felt . . . that you were in plain view." Professors in turn called on the women more often than the men. Ginsburg recalled, "It wasn't harassment as much as it was fun and games: 'Let's call on the woman for comic relief.'"[16]

HARVARD LAW REVIEW

Despite these impediments, Ginsburg quickly distinguished herself as one of the most gifted students in her class. At the conclusion of her first year, she was named to the *Harvard Law Review*, fulfilling a prediction made by her greatest booster, Martin Ginsburg. She remarked:

> My husband is my biggest supporter. That was certainly true my first year in law school. Like all first-year law students, I had concerns about how I was doing in relation to all those brilliant people. My husband told his classmates and mine: "My wife is going to be on the *Law Review*."[17]

Most law schools publish a law review, a journal of legal scholarship with articles analyzing court proceedings, legislation, and the like. To be named to the staff of the law review is among the highest honors one can achieve as a legal student. Consequently, competition is fierce, especially at the top schools. To make law review at Harvard as a mother in the 1950s was an altogether unprecedented accomplishment.

Of course, while law review was an honor, it was also a demanding assignment, with additional responsibilities and long hours. Ginsburg would bring Jane to work at the publication's offices in Harvard's Gannett House. Now a toddler, Jane would follow her mother around while she worked. For her singular work ethic and fierce determination, her classmates, who marveled at her ambition and grace, dubbed Ginsburg "Ruthless Ruthie." In a compelling tribute to her, Ronald Loeb, a fellow student, declared:

> While the rest of us were sulking around in dirty khaki pants and frayed button-down Oxford shirts, missing classes and complaining about all the work we had, you set a standard too high for any of us to achieve: you never missed classes; you were always prepared; your *Law Review* work was always done; you were always beautifully dressed and impeccably groomed; and you had a happy husband and a lovely young daughter.[18]

CANCER STRIKES AGAIN

Unfortunately, in Ginsburg's second year of law school, cancer again threatened to take the life of someone very dear to her. In his final year of study at Harvard, Martin was diagnosed with cancer of the lymphatic system. His prognosis was not good: doctors thought his chances for survival were slim. In the words of Ruth's cousin Jane Gervitz, the cancer "was like a sword hanging over their heads."[19] Ginsburg recollected, "We made a decision to take one day at a time. We never had a defeatist attitude. We were going to get through."[20] Martin underwent two major surgeries as well as radiation treatment, which made him profoundly sick for weeks at a time. Despite Martin's illness, the law school administration would not give him additional time to complete his assignments or adjust the requirements necessary for graduation. So the Ginsburgs arranged for others to attend his classes and take notes, which they later shared with Martin. Ginsburg herself sat in for him on occasion, while still attending to her own responsibilities, and helped him write his final paper. Their determination paid off, and not only did Martin beat cancer, that he managed to complete his senior year and graduate on time with Harvard Law's class of 1958.

NEW YORK CITY AND COLUMBIA LAW SCHOOL

Martin Ginsburg accepted a position at the firm of Weil, Gotshal, & Manges in New York City. Rather than have the family live apart for a year, Ruth transferred to Columbia University School of Law, also in the Big Apple. News of Ginsburg's arrival preceded her. At Harvard, she was on the law review and ranked near the very top of her class, so the students at Columbia were worried. "We had heard," remarked Nina Appel, one of her classmates at Columbia, "that the smartest person on the East Coast was going to transfer, and that we were all going to drop down one rank."[21] As it turned out, those fears were well placed. Not only did Ginsburg make *Columbia Law Review*, but she graduated in a tie for first in Columbia University School of Law's class of 1959. At the graduation festivities, when Ginsburg walked across the dais to receive her degree, Jane Ginsburg proudly shouted for the whole audience to hear, "That's my Mommy!"[22]

Lawyer and Professor

Despite her stellar record in law school, Ruth Bader Ginsburg did not receive any job offers upon graduating from Columbia. She applied to many private firms and for a number of clerkships in U.S. District Court, but no one hired her. The large firm where she worked during her summers off from school decided not to keep her on permanently: "I thought I had done a terrific job and I expected them to offer me a job on graduation."[1] Yet she recalled, "Not a single law firm in the entire city of New York bid for my employment."[2]

That a Columbia Law graduate ranked first in her class and a member of the law review at both Harvard and Columbia could not find a position was a curious situation. But there were a number of reasons for Ginsburg's lack of luck. "In the fifties the traditional law firms were just beginning to turn around on hiring Jews," she observed. "They had just gotten over that form of discrimination. But to be a woman, a Jew, and a mother to boot, that combination was a bit much."[3] In hindsight, Ginsburg felt that the main sticking point for potential employers was that she had a child, which they assumed would prevent her from focusing fully on her duties as an attorney.

Still, she refused to accept defeat or give in to bitterness. "I don't think that being angry or being hostile is very productive," she said, since to change people's minds "you have to do it through constant dialogue, constant persuasion, and not in shouting matches."[4] A year after Ginsburg's graduation, a professor she knew at Harvard recommended her for a clerkship in the office of Felix Frankfurter, a justice on the U.S. Supreme Court. A Supreme Court clerkship is among the most sought-after opportunities for law school graduates, and Ginsburg was excited by the possibility. Yet, though Frankfurter was Jewish and had hired the first African-American clerk in 1948, he hesitated at offering the post to a woman. "Does she wear skirts?" he reportedly asked. "I can't stand girls in pants."[5] Ginsburg never interviewed with Frankfurter and her job search continued.

A CLERKSHIP

Finally, Judge Edmund L. Palmieri, who served on the U.S. District Court for the Southern District of New York, hired Ginsburg to clerk for him—only after being repeatedly reassured by one of her professors at Columbia that she could handle the dual responsibilities of motherhood and the clerkship. Given her long and difficult job search, she dedicated all her talent to succeeding in the position. For the next two years, she recalled, "I worked harder than any other law clerk in the building, stayed late whenever it was necessary, sometimes when it wasn't necessary, came

As a young lawyer, Ruth Bader Ginsburg sought a clerkship with Felix Frankfurter, a justice on the U.S. Supreme Court. Despite her qualifications, Frankfurter was uncomfortable with giving such a position to a woman.

in Saturdays, and brought work home."[6] The high quality of Ginsburg's work soon persuaded Palmieri that he had made the right choice, and the two quickly became friends. Their mutual respect and admiration endured long after the clerkship ended. Palmieri rated Ginsburg one of the five best clerks he ever had, while she described him as "a man I deeply admired, whose friendship I cherished to this day."[7]

As at law school, Ginsburg could not have dedicated so much of her time and energy to her work if not for Martin. As a tax attorney, he had a demanding job too, but unlike most men his age, rather than leave the housework and childrearing to his wife, he shared in the responsibilities. So that he would not have to spend as much time at the office, he acquired a large legal library to keep at home, so he could work while looking after Jane.

During her clerkship with Judge Palmieri, Ginsburg received some insight into why she had been repeatedly turned down in her search for legal work. Palmieri chauffeured Learned Hand, a renowned federal judge, to his office every day and Ginsburg often came along. She had applied for a clerkship with Hand but was not hired. During one of their trips, Hand explained that he had not given her the job because he felt she might find his language offensive. Ginsburg responded that he did not censor his language when they were driving together and wondered what the difference was. Hand replied, "Young lady, here I am not looking you in the face."[8]

OFF TO SWEDEN

In 1961, at the conclusion of her two-year clerkship with Judge Palmieri, Ginsburg found herself recruited by a number of potential employers, a welcome change from her initial job search. With Palmieri's recommendation, she received job offers at law firms and for academic positions. After careful thought, Ginsburg opted for a two-year stint with the International Procedure Project at Columbia Law School, working under Professor Hans Smit. Her assignment was to study the judicial system and legal procedures in Sweden and author a book about it. As to why she chose academic work over private practice, she remarked:

During her long search for a job, Ruth Bader Ginsburg also applied for a clerkship with Learned Hand, a respected federal judge. Hand was unwilling to give her a position because he felt his language was too coarse for a young woman to hear.

I did that for a few reasons, some clear to me then, others probably locked in my subconscious. One reason was the opportunity to write a book. . . .

Another attractive feature was going off to a foreign land I knew nothing about and being wholly on my own.[9]

To begin her work, she spent several months learning the Swedish language in preparation for the two research trips she would take to Sweden over the next two years. Her first stay there lasted four months, most of which was spent as a research associate in the city of Lund. For several weeks during her summer vacation, Jane kept her mother company, and Martin flew in for a visit as well. Throughout her studies in Sweden, Ginsburg was struck by the country's approach to child care. As she recalled, "The University of Lund, where I did much of my work, had a fine day-care center for children of students and faculty, just an excellent place. That kind of all-day center was just about unknown in the United States then."[10] Jane accompanied her mother for the entire two months of her second trip to Sweden. Now an associate director for the project, Ginsburg conducted her research in Stockholm, while Jane attended a Swedish children's camp south of the city. During her stay, Ginsburg was repeatedly impressed by the advances Swedish women had made, especially in the workplace. Though she had endured sexist discrimination throughout her academic career, Ginsburg never described herself as a feminist. Now, however, after seeing how much women had progressed in Sweden as compared to the United States, she started to develop a more feminist outlook.

With her research complete, Ginsburg returned to New York in 1963 to finish writing her book. Only 10 years old, Jane still managed to help proofread the manuscript. "My 'professional association' with my mother began at a very early age,"[11] Jane quipped. Co-authored by Ginsburg and Anders Bruzelius, *Civil Procedure in Sweden* consisted of two volumes and was released in 1965 by a Dutch publisher

The Supreme Court in Stockholm, Sweden, where Ruth Bader Ginsburg spent two years studying the legal system of that European nation in the early 1960s.

in association with the Parker School of Foreign and Comparative Law at Columbia.

TEACHING AT RUTGERS LAW

Having completed her work for the International Procedure Project, Ginsburg needed to figure out the next step in her career. Rutgers School of Law in Newark, New Jersey, would provide the answer. After an African-American faculty member resigned, Rutgers—known for its progressive hiring practices—sought to recruit another black professor to take his place. When the school could not find a suitable candidate, they decided to offer the post to a woman instead, and Ginsburg filled the bill. She accepted their offer and joined the faculty as an assistant professor. "I never thought it would be possible for me to be a law professor," she commented. "There were only half a dozen women law professors across the country. I didn't want to teach that early. I wanted to be an advocate for four years or so, but such an opportunity wouldn't come again. I took what I could get."[12]

Ginsburg became one of the first 20 women to teach at a law school in the United States. As luck would have it, there was already a woman on staff at Rutgers Law, so she was not entirely alone. As at Cornell and both Harvard and Columbia law schools, Ginsburg had gained entry to an institution that had long been dominated by men, yet despite Rutgers's seemingly progressive hiring practices, old habits died hard. When she joined the Rutgers faculty, Ginsburg was informed that she would receive less money than her male counterparts. She recalled, "The good dean of the law school carefully explained about the state university's limited resources and then added it was only fair to pay me modestly because my husband had a very good job."[13] Years later, she and other women on the faculty filed a lawsuit against the university for violating the Equal Pay Act and compelled Rutgers to pay them their fair share.

For the next nine years, from 1963 to 1971, Ginsburg taught legal procedure to law students at Rutgers. The experience was a pleasant one: "I found I liked teaching. I liked the sense of being my own boss. . . . There's tremendous luxury in being a law teacher in that you can spend most of your time doing whatever interests you."[14] Ginsburg was popular with her students. Regarding her teaching philosophy, she commented:

I don't pretend to be neutral on issues when I am not. I like the students to understand that most of us have a perspective, most thinking people do, but that it's important to disclose one's biases. I'm not trying to brainwash people, but I'm not going to present myself as neutral. I don't think my students have any doubt where I stand on the Bill of Rights.[15]

JAMES STEVEN GINSBURG

On September 8, 1965, Ginsburg gave birth to a son, James Steven Ginsburg. The pregnancy was unexpected—the couple had been told 10 years earlier that they could not have any more children—and also posed a bit of a problem for Ginsburg, who had not forgotten what the news of her first pregnancy had meant for her position at the Social Security office in Oklahoma. Adding to her worry was the fact that she did not have tenure at Rutgers but was instead signing individual one-year contracts. She worried that if her superiors learned of her condition, they would not renew her contract, potentially damaging her career. So during the first months of her pregnancy, she disguised her condition with oversized clothing. By the time she could no longer hide it, Rutgers had already renewed her contract. James's birth was well timed, and Ginsburg only had to miss a couple of weeks of class before returning to her teaching duties.

With a newborn, a daughter in grade school, a husband, and a flourishing teaching career, Ginsburg had considerable responsibilities. When her aging father moved in for a number of months to recover from a car accident not long after James was born, she had even more things to manage. However, as she had at every stage of her life, when confronted with these seemingly impossible challenges, she found a way to persevere. With her husband's help, she juggled her responsibilities—staying up late to grade papers, surviving on three or four hours of sleep a night, or catching up on her reading while riding the train back and forth to Newark. Ginsburg's efforts were rewarded when she was promoted to associate professor at Rutgers. In 1969, Rutgers made her a full professor and awarded her tenure—one of the principle goals of any professor. It means that the professor can stay on at the school for as long as he or she likes. In the late 1960s, there were very few female law professors with tenure. Once again, Ginsburg was blazing her own path.

Still, like any family, the Ginsburgs endured their share of conflicts. Independent from an early age, Jane did not always excel in school. She admitted, "I didn't have many friends, and my behavior was very bad."[16] Once in a while a negative conduct report found its way to Martin and Ruth, who were strict disciplinarians. Mostly it was left to Martin to carry out the punishments, banning television and the like. "When I did something bad," Jane reminisced, "my mother would be real quiet. While Dad was more vocal and demonstrative, Mom was aggressively disappointed."[17] Given her parents' work schedules, Jane certainly had cause to resent their absence yet felt nothing of the sort. "I think I rather enjoyed my situation. Since I was alone so much, I had more freedom. I got away with a lot."[18]

Perhaps Ginsburg's most challenging day as a parent came when James was only two years old. At Rutgers, she received a distraught phone call from the family nanny, who told her that James had swallowed some drain cleaner stored under the kitchen sink. The nanny had rushed him to the hospital, where he was being treated for burns. When Martin and Ruth arrived, they received a terrible shock— chemical burns covered much of James's face. "Charred lips encircled his mouth—a tiny, burnt-out cavern, ravaged by the lye,"[19] Ginsburg remembered with horror. Doctors informed them that the burns—to the face, mouth, and throat—were potentially fatal. Over the next several days, the doctors worked to save his life. James survived, but the chemicals left behind severe scars. Thanks to a series of reconstructive surgeries, however, James avoided any lasting disfigurement.

Though her son came out of the ordeal with his life and without any major damage to his face, Ginsburg wrestled with a sense of guilt, feeling that in some way her decision to focus on her career was to blame for the mishap. Whatever her momentary doubts had been at the time, her children credit both her and Martin with creating a fulfilling home life for them. "The family was always home for dinner," James recalled. "And a night did not go by when my mother did not check to see that I was doing my schoolwork. She was always there when I wanted her to be—and even when I didn't."[20]

The ACLU's Women's Rights Project

It was during her time at Rutgers that Ruth Bader Ginsburg first became involved in the women's rights movement and with the American Civil Liberties Union (ACLU). Motivated by the discrimination she had endured throughout her career and inspired by such feminist texts as *The Second Sex* by French author Simone de Beauvoir, Ginsburg sought to use the law to correct gender-based injustice. "Both the ACLU and my students prodded me to take an active part in the effort to eliminate senseless gender lines in the law," Ginsburg stated. "Once I became involved, I found the legal work fascinating and had high hopes for significant change in the next decade."[1]

REED V. REED: THE GRANDMOTHER BRIEF

At first, the New Jersey branch of the ACLU referred gender-based discrimination cases to Ginsburg. Then, in 1971, she served as the main author of a legal brief on behalf of the ACLU to the U.S. Supreme Court in the case of *Reed v. Reed*. The law being challenged in the case was a statute in Idaho that gave preferential treatment to men in handling the estates of deceased family members and friends. In this case, Sally Reed of Boise was denied permission to administer the estate of her deceased son in favor of her ex-husband, even though she had applied first. The law stated rather bluntly, "Males must be preferred to females."[2] Ginsburg contended that the law assumed that men were better able to deal with the responsibility of handling an estate and argued—in what became known as the "grandmother brief," as it would later be used in many women's rights cases—that the statute in question violated the Equal Protection Clause of the Fourteenth Amendment to the Constitution. The Fourteenth Amendment holds that, among other things, "No State shall make or enforce any law which shall abridge the privileges or immunities of citizens of the United States; nor shall any State deprive any person of life, liberty, or property, without due process of law; nor deny to any person within its jurisdiction the equal protection of the laws."

The Supreme Court agreed with Ginsburg. Chief Justice Warren Burger, in a unanimous 7–0 decision, wrote:

> To give a mandatory preference to members of either sex over members of the other, merely to accomplish the elimination of hearings on the merits, is to make the very kind of arbitrary legislative choice forbidden by the Equal Protection Clause of

the Fourteenth Amendment . . . [T]he choice in this context may not lawfully be mandated solely on the basis of sex.[3]

The ruling marked an extraordinary change in women's rights law. As Ginsburg observed, the decision "was the first time the Supreme Court ever overturned a law in response to a woman's complaint of unfair sex-based discrimination."[4] Sally Reed herself noted the importance of the verdict: "We never dreamed it would go this far. I just cared about the principle of the thing. . . . I hope more women will do what I did. Instead of complaining about the way things are, we've got to go into the courts and get them changed."[5]

THE ACLU

During World War I, many Americans who voiced their opposition to the conflict were jailed, persecuted, or otherwise silenced by the government. In response, in 1917, a group of leading civil libertarians, among them Roger Baldwin, Crystal Eastman, Albert DeSilver, and Norman Thomas, founded the National Civil Liberties Bureau to protect freedom of speech and the other rights set forth in the Constitution from assault by the government. Renamed the American Civil Liberties Union (ACLU) in 1920, the organization has played an important if controversial role in the American legal system in the decades since.

In the 1920s alone, the ACLU famously aided in the defense of Ferdinando Nicola Sacco and Bartolomeo Vanzetti, two Italian radicals accused of murdering a police officer, as well as helped challenge a Tennessee law that forbade the teaching of the theory of evolution in schools, which culminated in the famous Scopes "Monkey Trial" of 1925.

BACK AT COLUMBIA

Ginsburg left Rutgers Law in 1971 for a teaching assignment at Harvard Law School. Her time at Harvard was brief, however; in 1972, Columbia Law School offered her a full professorship. She accepted and became the first woman to not only serve as a full-time member of the faculty but also the first to receive tenure. Ginsburg would remain at Columbia, teaching constitutional law and civil procedure, until 1980. While there, in addition to working with students in the classroom, she was a founding counsel of the ACLU's Women's Rights Project (WRP). Through the WRP, Ginsburg would help to change the course of American legal history.

During her first few weeks at Columbia, Ginsburg waded into a gender discrimination incident. The school

While the ACLU is often seen as a liberal organization, the group has defended the civil liberties of right- and left-wing groups alike, siding with the National Rifle Association (NRA) in a legal dispute with the federal government, for example. Neither has the ACLU hesitated to protect the liberties of even the most hateful people and organizations, at one time even standing up in support of the American Nazi Party's right to hold a demonstration.

The ACLU is widely unpopular, especially among conservatives, because the organization often has defended gay rights, abortion rights, and the rights of accused criminals or terrorists. The ACLU's three-pronged strategy of public education, legislative lobbying, and litigation has dramatically influenced the American legal system. Indeed, other than the federal government itself, no organization has participated in as many Supreme Court cases as the ACLU.

had instituted a round of layoffs, cutting several cleaning ladies but leaving the janitorial staff—all men—untouched. However, "I entered the fray," Ginsburg recollected, "which

IN HER OWN WORDS

In an interview with the *New York Times*, Ruth Bader Ginsburg recalled her time at Columbia:

I was the first tenured woman at Columbia. That was 1972, every law school was looking for its woman. Why? Because Stan Pottinger, who was then head of the office for civil rights of the Department of Health, Education and Welfare, was enforcing the Nixon government contract program. Every university had a contract, and Stan Pottinger would go around and ask, How are you doing on your affirmative-action plan? A reporter asked William McGill, who was then the president of Columbia: How is Columbia doing with its affirmative action? He said, It's no mistake that the two most recent appointments to the law school are a woman and an African-American man. . . . I was the woman. I never would have gotten that invitation from Columbia without the push from the Nixon administration. I understand that there is a thought that people will point to the affirmative-action baby and say she couldn't have made it if she were judged solely on the merits. But when I got to Columbia I was well regarded by my colleagues even though they certainly disagreed with many of the positions that I was taking. They backed me up: If that's what I thought, I should be able to speak my mind.*

---

* Emily Bazelon, "The Place of Women on the Court," *New York Times*. July 7, 2009, http://www.nytimes.com/2009/07/12/magazine/12ginsburg-t.html.

happily ended with no layoffs, and, as I recall, the union's first female shop steward."[6]

THE WRP

Based on the success of the *Reed* decision, the board of directors of the ACLU voted to establish the WRP in 1972. The WRP's purpose was to battle gender-based discrimination in the courts. At the WRP's inception, Ginsburg was named co-director with Brenda Feigen Fasteau, who would manage the WRP's operations while Ginsburg would focus on the actual litigation. In 1973, Ginsburg was named general counsel to the ACLU, and then named to the organization's board of directors in 1974. For the WRP, "Our idea was to try to find the right cases, bring them before the most sympathetic tribunals, and help develop constitutional law in the gender classification area step by step,"[7] Ginsburg stated.

With her roles as a law professor and co-director of the WRP, not to mention as a wife and mother, Ginsburg once again was required to multitask. During the 1970s, numerous gender discrimination suits were being filed in the courts, in part because women were entering the workforce in record numbers. In so doing, they found that they were not always treated equally. With so many suits being filed, however, the courts did not know which ones to hear. The WRP, in turn, sought to elevate only the cases they thought they could win in the courts. Regarding the WRP's strategy, Ginsburg and Fasteau focused on cases in six specific areas of the law, areas which they thought could get them fair hearings in court: birth control (but not abortion rights), admissions to educational institutions, government training programs, employment-related issues, government aid to private entities, and discrimination in lending. During her eight years on the WRP, Ginsburg was involved in a total of 34 Supreme Court cases, arguing six as either lead or co-counsel. Of these six, Ginsburg won five. Recalling those days, Kathleen Peratis, a staff director on the project, remarked, "It was a heady time. We won everything. We thought it would never end."[8]

FRONTIERO V. RICHARDSON

On January 17, 1973, Ginsburg argued her first case before the Supreme Court on behalf of the WRP. Oddly enough, in the case in question, *Frontiero v. Richardson*, the injured party was a man. This was a common strategy in Ginsburg's work for the WRP. In order to break down gender discrimination, she would take on statutes that on the surface seemed to benefit women but in truth reinforced what she believed were harmful gender stereotypes. Her goal was to show that these stereotypes hurt men just as much as they hurt women. In the *Frontiero* case, an Air Force lieutenant, Sharron Frontiero, and her husband, Joseph, sued Secretary of Defense Eliot L. Richardson over a law that made it easier for the wives of military men to claim dependent benefits than for the husbands of military women. Under the statute, wives with husbands in the military were automatically treated as dependents, whether they needed their husbands' income or not. For a husband whose wife was in the armed services to claim the benefits, however, the wife had to prove that she was responsible for more than half of his financial support. The underlying assumption of the law was that women were dependent on their husbands but not vice versa. "Women," Ginsburg argued, "were branded inferior through such treatment."[9] Describing the strategic rationale for going forward with the *Frontiero* case, Ginsburg said, "We wanted to get rid of these gender labels in the law. *Frontiero* was a very good case to do that because it could easily be perceived as a straight equal pay case. Two people in the military, both the same rank, one gets more than the other."[10]

Presenting the case before the Supreme Court, Ginsburg did her best to overcome her anxiety. "I was terribly

A portrait of Ruth Bader Ginsburg taken in the mid-1970s, while she was serving as a professor at Columbia Law School in New York City and successfully arguing cases before the U.S. Supreme Court for the ACLU's Women's Rights Project.

nervous," she later stated. "In fact, I didn't eat lunch for fear that I might throw up. Two minutes into my argument, the fear dissolved. Suddenly, I realized that here before me were the nine leading jurists of America, a captive audience. I felt a surge of power that carried me through."[11] She concluded her argument to the court with a quote from Sarah Grimke, a women's rights pioneer in the 1800s. "I ask no favor for my sex. All I ask of our brethren is that they take their feet off our necks."[12]

The Supreme Court rendered its verdict on May 14, 1973, ruling 8–1 in favor of the Frontieros and the WRP. Writing for the majority, Justice William Brennan Jr. commented, "There can be no doubt that our nation has had a long and unfortunate history of sex discrimination. Traditionally, such discrimination was rationalized by an attitude of 'romantic paternalism' which, in practical effect, put women not on a pedestal but in a cage." Following the decision, Ginsburg characterized it as "the most far-reaching and important ruling on sex discrimination to come out of the Supreme Court yet. It will spell the beginning of reforms in hundreds of statutes which do not give equal benefits to men and women."[13] After *Frontiero*, the military changed its rules so that women and men were treated equally in determining dependent status.

KAHN V. SHEVIN

Ginsburg's next opportunity to bring a case before the Supreme Court came at the end of February 1974. In the case of *Kahn v. Shevin*, a Florida law allowed widows but not widowers a $500 deduction in their annual property taxes. As in *Frontiero*, Ginsburg saw the statute as an example of women being deemed inferior to men. The Supreme Court, however, did not agree. By a margin of 6–3, the Court ruled on April 24, 1974, that the purpose of the exemption was to improve the finances of women relative to men, to level the playing field between the genders, and thus was not discriminatory. Despite this setback, the *Kahn* decision did little to upset Ginsburg and the WRP's momentum, and before long they were back before the Supreme Court with another case.

WEINBERGER V. WIESENFELD

On January 20, 1975, in the *Weinberger v. Wiesenfeld* case, Ginsburg represented Stephen Wiesenfeld, a New Jersey widower who was seeking his deceased wife's Social Security benefits to help raise their infant son. Paula Wiesenfeld had been a schoolteacher and the family's primary source of income. The Social Security Administration had denied Wiesenfeld's claim because the Social Security Act only listed women as dependents, so men could not claim benefits based on their wives' employment. Ginsburg became aware of Wiesenfeld's plight through a letter he had written to a New Jersey newspaper in which he noted that had he been a woman and his wife a man, he would not have had to ask for help—the benefits would have come more or less automatically.

In Ginsburg's estimation, this was another instance of the law reflecting gender bias: Again women were assumed to be dependents, the men sources of income. In her argument before the court, Ginsburg sought "to show that the real issue was not a narrow women's rights question, but a question about people's freedom to organize their lives on the basis of their own judgment."[14] The law, she contended, "must deal with the parent, not the mother; with the homemaker, not the housewife; and with the surviving spouse, not the widow."[15] Ginsburg's reasoning carried the day, and on March 19, 1975, the court ruled unanimously, 8–0, that the law was unconstitutional.

ARTS AND LEISURE

A heavy workload did not keep Ginsburg from fulfilling her role as a parent or from enjoying her favorite pastimes. While managing litigation for the WRP, preparing and pleading her cases before the Supreme Court, and teaching law students as a full professor at one of the most prestigious law schools in the country, she still found time for her family—and for herself. The Ginsburgs made sure Jane and James experienced New York City's many cultural attractions. The New York Philharmonic orchestra, Broadway shows, children's theater—the family attended them all together. One pastime the Ginsburg children could not avoid was the opera. Because both Martin and Ruth were opera lovers, they frequently took their children to New York's Metropolitan Opera House.

Away from New York City, the Ginsburgs enjoyed more solitary pursuits. Avid boaters, they sailed on the Caribbean during their vacations. They also like to water-ski. An accomplished equestrian since her days at Camp Che-Na-Wah, Ginsburg passed her love of horseback riding to her son. And Martin did not give up his passion for golf after college—rather, the whole family took it up, with the future Supreme Court justice developing a peculiar yet effective style all her own. One guest in a tribute to her for Ginsburg's fiftieth birthday compared it to her political leanings, observing, "She stands left, swings right, and hits straight down the middle."[16]

CRAIG V. BOREN

In the case of *Craig v. Boren*, which was argued before the Supreme Court on October 5, 1976, Ginsburg targeted an Oklahoma law that permitted women to buy beer at 18 while men had to wait until they were 21. Here again, Ginsburg and the WRP sought to show how gender discrimination could harm men as well as women. The rationale behind the law was that men were more likely to drive after drinking, while women were assumed to be more responsible. In a 7–2 ruling on December 20, 1976, the Supreme Court found that the law was unconstitutional because it violated the Fourteenth Amendment's guarantee of equal protection.

With each appearance before the Supreme Court, Ginsburg gained confidence. As time wore on, the justices recognized her abilities and treated her with notable respect. Still, Ginsburg was naturally shy and preferred to make her case in writing rather than aloud. For inspiration and motivation, she would remember her mother. "When I argue before the . . . Court, I wear her earrings and her pin and I think how pleased she would be if she were there."[17]

In her presentations, Ginsburg was firm but soft-spoken, often taking long pauses so that the effect of her words could fully resonate. She kept her emotions under control and always came to court meticulously prepared, with a strategic vision of how to win the case. "Her work was very clear, very orderly," one observer noted. "She never guessed, she never weaseled, she was always thoroughly prepared. She always knew all the facts and all the laws of every case she cited."[18]

CALIFANO V. GOLDFARB

Not long after *Craig v. Boren*, Ginsburg and the WRP took on the Social Security Administration once again. Ginsburg represented Leon Goldfarb, an elderly widower who, following his wife's death, applied to receive survivor benefits from Social Security. He was denied because Hannah Goldfarb's pay accounted for less than 50 percent of the couple's total income. Were he a widow instead of a widower, however, Goldfarb would have received the benefits automatically, regardless of his deceased spouse's wages. Ginsburg saw similarities between *Califano v. Goldfarb* and

(continues on page 60)

THURGOOD MARSHALL

Thurgood Marshall was born on July 2, 1902, in Baltimore, Maryland. His father, a railroad porter, instilled in him a deep love of the U.S. Constitution, and after graduating in 1925 from Lincoln University, a historically black college in Pennsylvania, Marshall applied to law school at the University of Maryland. Though an exceptional student, he was denied admission because of his race. At the time, thanks to the 1896 Supreme Court case *Plessy v. Ferguson*, "separate but equal" was the law of the land, and African Americans could be barred from attending public schools with whites.

Supreme Court Justice Thurgood Marshall was the first African-American judge to serve on the nation's highest court.

While deeply hurt by this rejection, Marshall did not let this setback deter him. He instead went to Howard University School of Law in Washington, D.C., graduating at the top of his class in 1933. He then set up a civil rights legal practice in Baltimore and soon forced the University of Maryland School of Law to admit its first black student. Marshall joined the National Association for the Advancement of Colored People (NAACP), eventually moving to New York before becoming the organization's national counsel in 1938.

In 1939, Marshall helped establish the NAACP Legal Defense and Educational Fund (LDF) to fight segregation in education. Over the next 22 years, as director and chief counsel of the LDF, he argued 32 cases before the U.S. Supreme Court, winning 29 of them. But education was not his only focus; he also led a general assault on the Jim Crow system of racial segregation, taking on discrimination in voting rights, housing, and other areas. His most famous victory came in the 1954 case of *Brown v. Board of Education*, in which the Court unanimously overthrew the "separate but equal" system of education that had been practiced since *Plessy v. Ferguson*.

In 1961, President John F. Kennedy nominated Marshall to the U.S Court of Appeals for the Second Circuit, but it would be a year before he could take his seat, as supporters of segregation in the U.S. Senate held up his confirmation. Marshall served on the Second Circuit until 1965, when he became solicitor general of the United States following his nomination by President Lyndon B. Johnson. As solicitor general, Marshall argued 19 cases before the Supreme Court on behalf of the federal government, winning 14 of them.

After his nomination by President Johnson, on August 13, 1967, Thurgood Marshall became the first African-American justice of the U.S. Supreme Court, where he served for the next 34 years. In his early days on the Court, Marshall was part of a broad liberal majority led by Chief Justice Earl Warren that expanded civil liberties, as well as judicial and federal powers, in ways not previously seen. However, President Richard Nixon and President Ronald Reagan remade the Court, appointing conservative jurists who shifted it decidedly to the right,

(continues)

(continued)

leaving Marshall in the minority on many decisions. In 1991, his health failing, Marshall was forced to resign his post despite his grave worries about the direction of the Court. A conservative, Clarence Thomas, also an African American, was named to replace him. Two years later, on January 24, 1993, Thurgood Marshall died.

(continued from page 57)

some of her earlier cases, describing it as "*Wiesenfeld* minus the baby," or "*Frontiero* with a heftier price tag."[19] On March 2, 1977, the Supreme Court ruled 5–4 in favor of Leon Goldfarb. Justice Brennan, writing for the majority, declared that the Social Security Administration's action "results in the efforts of female workers required to pay social security taxes producing less protection for their spouses than is produced by the efforts of male workers,"[20] and was thus unconstitutional.

DUREN V. MISSOURI

In the last case Ginsburg argued before the Court, *Duren v. Missouri*, she advocated for a petitioner who had been convicted on criminal charges in a jury trial. Ginsburg questioned the jury selection system, which under a Missouri statute allowed women to easily claim an exemption so that they would not have to serve. Consequently, most juries were overwhelmingly male. Ginsburg contended that this violated the defendant's rights to a representative jury as guaranteed by the Sixth and Fourteenth amendments to the Constitution and held men and women to different standards of citizenship. Ginsburg presented her case on November 1, 1978. In an 8–1 decision issued on January 9, 1979, the Supreme Court concurred with Ginsburg and threw out the statute.

THE THURGOOD MARSHALL OF THE WOMEN'S RIGHTS MOVEMENT

The six cases Ginsburg argued before the Supreme Court only tell part of the story. In the 34 total cases in which she took part, she authored numerous amicus (supporting) briefs for attorneys working on other cases. Her efforts on behalf of the WRP earned her comparisons to Thurgood Marshall, the famed civil rights attorney and later Supreme Court justice who helped construct the legal framework of civil rights through litigation by persuading the courts to strike down laws that arbitrarily differentiated between blacks and whites. Ginsburg used a similar strategy in support of women's rights and gender equality with the WRP. She "had a real vision of where she wanted to go and what she had to do to get there," Kathleen Peratis recalled. "She is my idol. I named my daughter after her. I told my daughter that her namesake would be the first woman to sit on the Supreme Court. It turns out I was only off by one."[21]

In her near decade of service for the Women's Rights Project, Ruth Bader Ginsburg built an impressive legacy, cementing her place as one of the most significant litigators of the latter half of the twentieth century. Taken together, her many legal victories went a long way in breaking down the legal barriers between the sexes. With such impressive achievements, the only question was what her next step would be. In 1980, President Jimmy Carter provided the answer.

The U.S. Court of Appeals

It comes as little surprise that Ruth Bader Ginsburg—with her string of Supreme Court victories and her years as a law school professor at Rutgers and Columbia—eventually caught the attention of the White House. In 1980, when a seat opened up on the U.S. Court of Appeals for the District of Columbia Circuit, President Jimmy Carter nominated Ginsburg to fill it. The U.S. Senate voted to confirm her, and on June 30, 1980, Ginsburg took the oath of office to become only the second woman to serve on a federal appeals court.

A CAPITAL MOVE

With her new position, Ginsburg and her family moved from New York City to Washington, D.C., taking up

residence in a two-floor apartment in the Watergate building on the banks of the Potomac River. At 25, Jane Ginsburg
was already living on her own and was unaffected by the
relocation. A graduate of the University of Chicago, from
which she also received a master's degree, Jane followed in
her mother's footsteps and pursued a legal career, finishing
Harvard Law School not long before Ruth became a judge.
In fact, Jane and Ruth were the first mother-daughter duo
to gain entry to Harvard Law. Like her mother before her,
Jane also made the law review.

Martin Ginsburg made a smooth transition. Though he
was a professor at Columbia and had a thriving law practice
in New York City, he found plenty of work in Washington,
joining the faculty of Georgetown University Law Center,
where he taught tax law, and signing on to the Washington
office of the prestigious law firm of Fried, Frank, Harris,
Shriver, and Jacobson. At 15, James Ginsburg adjusted well
to Washington, D.C., taking advantage of the many opportunities the city had to offer.

ON THE BENCH

As one of 11 judges then on the D.C. Circuit, Ginsburg
had a new role to play. In her work on the WRP, she had
sought to move the law in a specific direction—toward a
greater recognition of gender equality. Now, however, she
had to dispassionately weigh the merits of a case and rule
according to the law as it was written, not how she thought
it should be written. "One of the most sacred duties of a
judge," Ginsburg stated, "is not to read her convictions
into the Constitution."[1] In cases that go before the D.C.
Circuit, a three-judge panel reviews them. Lawyers for the
plaintiffs and defendants submit briefs summarizing their
position and the grounds for either granting or denying
the appeal of the lower court's decision. The attorneys

Martin Ginsburg, Ruth Bader Ginsburg's husband, is photographed at home in Washington, D.C, in July 1993, shortly after her nomination to the Supreme Court. A progressive thinker who believed in the equality of the sexes, he made a name for himself as a preeminent tax attorney while sharing family and household duties with his wife.

sometimes also make oral arguments and respond to questions from the judges.

After considering the issues involved, the judges confer and vote on whether to uphold the lower court's decision or to overturn it. In this respect, they behave more like a jury than trial judges. The majority then writes an opinion describing their reasons for overturning or upholding the appeal. Since at least two of the three judges must agree on the opinion, a meeting of the minds must take place so that the decision is written in a way that the majority can sign on to it. As Ginsburg remarked, "No single court of appeals judge can carry the day in any case. To attract a second vote and establish durable law for the Circuit, a judge may find it necessary to moderate his or her own position, sometimes to be less bold, other times to be less clear."[2]

Ginsburg's efforts on behalf of the WRP were both inspired and informed by the powerful feelings aroused by the struggle for women's rights. As an advocate for gender equality, she did not shy away from appeals to emotion if she thought they would help her case. Once she became a judge, however, she assumed a different role. "On the bench," one observer noted that Ginsburg displayed "little of the passion that so fueled her earlier work."[3]

That is not to say she no longer promoted gender equality. In fact, during one case before the appeals court, one of the attorneys working on it requested a continuance—a delay—because his wife was pregnant and he wanted to take time off to care for the baby. The two men serving on the three-judge panel quickly denied the request. However, Ginsburg asked for a meeting with her two colleagues:

> I said, "Here is a man telling us that he is going to take care of the baby" and all the votes turned around. [Now there was some] consciousness that the job—taking care of children—can and should be a man's job. And when a man says he's doing it, his work as a parent should be respected fully.[4]

"THE MEANS, NOT THE ENDS"

Having been appointed by a Democratic president and having made her name with the WRP, Ginsburg, many observers anticipated, would be a reliable liberal vote on the court. Yet her decisions on the bench were not always so easy to predict. In fact, many departed significantly from the conventional liberal viewpoint. In a 1992 case, she came out in opposition to a government program in Washington, D.C. that reserved a certain portion of the city's contracts for minority-owned businesses. Ginsburg wrote that the

THE U.S. COURT OF APPEALS

In the American judicial system, the U.S. Supreme Court is the final arbiter of constitutional matters, having the last say on whether decisions made by the lower courts violate or adhere to the Constitution. Before a case arrives at the Supreme Court, it is first channeled through the various lower courts. The United States has a total of 94 judicial circuits through which cases progress. Cases in these 94 circuits are at the trial level, where evidence is presented and disputed, witnesses are called, etc. From these 94 judicial circuits, if a plaintiff or defendant feels he or she has not received a fair hearing, a case can be appealed to the U.S. Court of Appeals, which is the last stop before a case can advance to the Supreme Court. In other words, the U.S. Court of Appeals is the second-highest court in the land. The Court of Appeals—and the Supreme Court above it—generally do not rule on evidence, guilt, or innocence but on whether the law has been applied correctly. Of course, most cases decided by the U.S. Court of Appeals do not make it beyond that point. The Supreme Court takes up only a select few Court of Appeals cases, and an even smaller number are overturned. A decision by a Court of Appeals is national in scope; its mandate is not limited to the state in which it originated but applies to all states.

There are 13 such federal appeals courts. Of these, there are 11 regional "circuits" that hear cases arising in the various states law in question violated an earlier Supreme Court decision that held that before such contracts were awarded, it needed to be established that discrimination was taking place. The D.C. statute, Ginsburg contended, did not do that.

that compose each circuit. (For example, the First Circuit covers cases originating in Maine, Massachusetts, New Hampshire, Rhode Island, and Puerto Rico, while the Fifth Circuit deals with those coming out of Louisiana, Mississippi, and Texas.) Of the remaining two, there is the Court of Appeals for the Federal Circuit, which was created in 1982. The Federal Circuit reviews disputes from across the country, not from a particular region, but it focuses primarily on trademark and patent cases and on those in which the federal government is the defendant. The U.S. Court of Appeals for the District of Columbia Circuit hears cases that develop in the nation's capital, a large share of them dealing with the federal government. There is also technically a fourteenth circuit, the U.S. Court of Appeals for the Armed Forces (CAAF), which exercises jurisdiction over American military personnel throughout the world.

While all federal appellate courts are equivalent in influence, the D.C. Circuit has long been viewed as first among equals in the sense that many of its rulings affect how various federal agencies operate; thus, its impact on government policy is considerable compared to the other circuits. In addition, many of the justices now serving on the Supreme Court were elevated from a position on the D.C. Circuit, among them Chief Justice John Roberts, Justice Clarence Thomas, and Justice Antonin Scalia.

The exceptional work ethic that Ginsburg developed over the course of her education and career as an attorney was one of her major strengths as a judge. She was always well prepared for every case that came before her, no matter how mundane. As Peter Huber, one of Ginsburg's former law clerks, wrote in a tribute to his former boss, "Lots of judges will give you their best on the grand legal [issues], like the First Amendment or equal protection. But with Ruth Ginsburg, it's the law itself that's grand. The means, not the ends. You see it in every opinion she writes, large or small." In particular, Huber recollected a number of trucking deregulation cases that he and Ginsburg had worked on in the early 1980s. Terrifically complicated and not terribly exciting, they were, for Huber, rather dreary work. Working with Ginsburg late into the night on one of the cases, he recalled how, surrounded by piles of files, Ginsburg "smiled a truly contented smile, a smile of deep pleasure and satisfaction, and said—with *complete* sincerity—'Peter, I think I've finally worked it out. This is an absolutely *fascinating* case.'"[5]

With clerks and colleagues alike, Ginsburg conducted herself with quiet grace and complete professionalism. Her clerks found her supportive and considerate but also quite demanding. A former law clerk named David Post observed that work he had submitted to her was returned "totally torn apart. Every word examined, literally. It was very painful. But I'll be forever in her debt, because that's what the law is—language."[6] Yet she also remembered her clerks' birthdays, scheduled annual reunions, and sponsored trips to the opera—or to the penitentiary so they could see how the less fortunate lived. A number of Ginsburg's clerks on the appeals court went on to clerk for Supreme Court justices, their work under Ginsburg having given them the skills to succeed at the next level.

As with her law clerks, Ginsburg demanded excellence from the attorneys that presented their cases before her.

Her questions were often pointed, sometimes catching lawyers off guard but also testing their preparation and the strengths of their arguments. Though she may have been tough in her dignified way, one attorney remarked, "I've never [heard] her raise her voice. She's absolutely the most polite judge."[7]

Among her colleagues on the appeals court, Ginsburg earned a sterling reputation during her 13 years on the bench. They marveled at her preparation, her grasp of the issues, and her well-reasoned decisions. Her demeanor was also an asset to the court. She was not an ideological bomb thrower, an approach that would have no doubt alienated her fellow judges. Rather, in her understated and quiet demeanor, she made her case and sought to convince rather than to shout down those who did not immediately agree with her. She became known as a consensus builder, a judge who did not add fuel to the fiery ideological battles that often take place on the bench. As Peter Huber stated, she "knows how to disagree without being disagreeable and has mastered the art so well she pulls people her way."[8]

In Ginsburg's view, a good judge "strives to persuade and not to pontificate. She speaks in a moderate and restrained voice, engaging in a dialogue with, not a diatribe against, co-equal departments of government, state authorities, and even her own colleagues."[9] On the appeals court, Ginsburg played this role well, relying on precedent and the law as it was written and considering each case on its individual merits and not through the prism of a political ideology, whether liberal or conservative.

THE GINSBURG FAMILY GROWS

As Ruth and Martin settled into their life in Washington, D.C., in 1981, their daughter, Jane, was married to George Spera Jr., who, like Jane, worked as a lawyer. After receiving her law degree from Harvard in 1980, Jane served a judicial clerkship and then joined a law firm in New York City. In 1985, Jane was the recipient of a prestigious Fulbright Award to study overseas. Accompanied by George, she moved to Paris, France, where George found a job in the Paris office of an American legal firm. At the Université de Paris II, she studied for her D.E.A., the French equivalent of a master's degree, which she earned in 1985. (Jane's Harvard pedigree is not the only trait she shares with her mother. She also followed in Ruth's footsteps as a law professor, taking up a post at her mother's former employer, Columbia Law School.)

In 1986, Jane gave birth to Paul Bertrand Spera, Ruth and Martin's first grandchild, in Paris. Unfortunately the birth was not without complications, and Jane suffered through a difficult recovery. As she regained her strength, Jane found comfort in her telephone conversations with her mother. Ruth recalled:

> It was not a good time at all. [Jane] called me from the hospital, and we talked for two hours. I remember telling her that soon this baby will love you more than anyone in the world. And when we'd hung up, I thought, "Gee, I must have done something right as a parent. When my daughter was feeling really low, she didn't call a friend. She called me. She called her mother."[10]

Jane and Paul had another child, a daughter named Clara Simone Spera, in 1990.

After finishing high school, James Ginsburg went on to the University of Chicago, the same school his sister had attended. Following his graduation, he embarked on a career in the music industry, working for classical music record labels.

Unfortunately, during Ruth's tenure on the Court of Appeals, Martin's health began to falter, and they soon learned that he would require heart surgery. He received a triple bypass in 1987. The procedure was a success and Martin's health improved. Still he suffered from a bad back, which forced the Ginsburgs to cut back on their golfing.

Having made a successful transition from New York City to Washington, D.C., and from a crusading law professor to a highly respected judge on the U.S. Court of Appeals, Ruth Bader Ginsburg had left an indelible mark on the legal profession in the United States. Had she retired in 1992, history would have regarded her highly, her work taught in classrooms and studied by attorneys. However, with the election of a Democratic president, Bill Clinton, that year, one more rung had been added to the ladder Ginsburg had been climbing. Whether she would be called on to take that final step, only time would tell.

To the Supreme Court

Early in President Bill Clinton's first term, Byron R. White, one of the nine justices then serving on the U.S. Supreme Court, announced his retirement. The vacancy offered Clinton the opportunity to remake the court. Appointed by President John F. Kennedy in 1962, White had disappointed many on the political left for his stances on affirmative action and abortion, among other issues. Indeed, in the highly controversial 1973 *Roe v. Wade* decision—in which the justices, by a 7–2 margin, upheld a woman's right to an abortion by citing an implied right to privacy embedded in the Constitution—White had written a powerful dissent.

In the years since 1973, the Supreme Court had become far more conservative. Supreme Court justices such as

Antonin Scalia and Clarence Thomas looked with skepticism not only on the legality of abortion rights but also on certain aspects of civil rights, criminal rights, and personal privacy, among other areas of the law. Consequently, with the departure of a right-of-center judge like White, Clinton could move the balance of the court back to the left. But he had to proceed carefully. His nominee needed to be approved by a majority of the U.S. Senate, which was never a sure thing, especially in the past decade. In the 1980s and early 1990s, Supreme Court nominees often faced bruising confirmation battles, as conservative and liberal politicians sought to discern a potential justice's political leanings. The confirmation hearings of Robert Bork, a Ronald Reagan nominee ultimately rejected by the Senate, and Clarence Thomas, a George H.W. Bush nominee who was narrowly approved, were notorious for their partisanship and the bad feelings they generated. Many Republicans with memories of those confirmation fights wanted to return the favor with Clinton's nominee. To avoid a repeat of the drama of the Bork and Thomas hearings, Clinton would have to find the perfect candidate, one with a résumé and reputation that were beyond reproach.

A LONG SEARCH COMMENCES

In his three-month search for Byron White's replacement, the president considered more than 40 candidates. What he sought, he stated, was someone with "a fine mind, good judgment, wide experience in the law and the problems of real people, and someone with a big heart."[1] Among his first choices was Governor Mario Cuomo of New York. A fiercely eloquent liberal, Cuomo had never served as a judge, but this was not unheard of for Supreme Court nominees. (Chief Justice Earl Warren, one of the most historically significant members of the Court, had arrived there after serving as governor of California.) Cuomo, however, was intent on an ill-fated run for a fourth term as governor and turned down the president. As the search continued, Clinton's popularity plummeted due to Cabinet confirmation fights, a long-sputtering economy, controversy over gays in the military, and other issues, sapping his political strength and further limiting whom he could choose to serve on the Court. He considered Bruce Babbitt, his secretary of the interior, but environmentalists wanted Babbitt to remain at his post, while Republicans vowed to fight his nomination. Clinton also contemplated nominating his secretary of education, Richard Riley, but Riley took himself out of the running.

Clinton then shifted his focus to two appeals court judges, interviewing Stephen Breyer, who served on the U.S. Court of Appeals for the First Circuit, in Boston, Massachusetts, and Ruth Bader Ginsburg. As it turned out, Clinton had met Ginsburg during the previous decade when he served as governor of Arkansas. Ginsburg had made a speech at the University of Arkansas Law School in Little Rock, after which she spoke with the young governor and met his wife, Hillary Rodham Clinton. Ginsburg came away struck by Clinton's charm but had not spoken with him since.

SETTLING ON A NOMINEE

Looking over the judge's record, Clinton was impressed by Ginsburg's calm in the face of the ideological battles that had been fought in the courts over the years. She had earned a reputation as a consensus builder and won the respect of her conservative colleagues for her evenhanded approach to the law. She did not let ideological differences affect her personal relationships, enjoying a deep friendship with Antonin Scalia, who served with her on the D.C. Court of Appeals before being elevated to the Supreme Court. With the Supreme Court deeply divided, Clinton could see that Ginsburg might help ease the partisanship while steering the Court in a more progressive direction.

Intrigued by the prospect of Ginsburg on the Supreme Court, Clinton ran her name by Senator Orrin Hatch of Utah, who was an important Republican member of the Senate Judiciary Committee, which would review any Supreme Court nomination before it went to a full vote in the Senate. Hatch approved of Ginsburg without reservation.

Clinton's aides got in touch with Ginsburg over the phone, inquiring about her background and where she would be in the weeks ahead, in order to set up a possible interview with the president. In the meantime, Clinton met with another prospect, Stephen Breyer, who, recovering from a recent cycling accident, did not particularly impress the president. Clinton had his staff call Ginsburg, who was attending a wedding in Vermont, to ask her to return to Washington to meet with him. Rather than hastily depart the wedding and perhaps create suspicions, the Ginsburgs flew back to the capital the following day.

On June 13, 1993, Ginsburg met with the president for more than an hour. Clinton, a Yale law graduate and a former legal professor, questioned Ginsburg about her involvement in the WRP and displayed an enthusiasm and engagement that impressed Ginsburg. During their conversation, Clinton asked her why he should name her to the Court. A humble Ginsburg replied, "I never thought I'd be here, sitting in front of the president of the United States talking about whether I should be on the Supreme Court."[2] After returning home from her interview, Ginsburg was beset by government attorneys who came to comb over the family tax returns. Ever the accomplished chef, Martin Ginsburg prepared a lunch for the guests.

Several hours later, at about 11:30 that evening, the president called Ginsburg from the White House residence and offered her the nomination. Ginsburg accepted and the two set about preparing for the next day's announcement in the Rose Garden.

Following the Rose Garden festivities, the Ginsburgs were subjected to a media onslaught. Television cameras became a part of their daily lives as Ginsburg prepared for her confirmation hearing before the 18 senators who comprised the Senate Judiciary Committee. Amid the congratulations that poured in from friends and well-wishers, interview requests, and other distractions, Ginsburg studied her writings and more than 300 legal decisions over the past decades and watched video recordings of recent confirmation hearings to see what worked and what did not for other Supreme Court nominees. She was aided in these preparations by White House staff and legal professors. Given her involvement with the ACLU, a frequent target of conservatives, the White House feared that Republicans would make an issue of her work for the WRP and for serving on the board of the ACLU. So in Ginsburg's preparation sessions, participants playing Republican questioners continually asked her to justify some of the ACLU's more controversial actions. Ever loyal to the organization, Ginsburg soon grew exasperated. "Stop it," she said. "There's nothing you can do to make me bad-mouth the ACLU."[3]

CONFIRMATION HEARINGS

Ginsburg's nomination hearing before the Senate Judiciary Committee commenced on July 20, 1993, and lasted three days. With millions watching on television, Ginsburg took her seat before the committee as many friends and family members looked on from the audience.

In her opening statement, Ginsburg thanked President Clinton for nominating her: "The president's confidence in my capacity to serve as a Supreme Court Justice is responsible for the proceedings about to begin. There are no words to tell him what is in my heart. I can say simply this: if con-firmed, I will try in every way to justify his faith in me." She also showed a firm understanding of the gravity of the post to which she'd been nominated. "Supreme Court Justices are guardians of the great charter that has served as our nation's fundamental instrument of government for over 200 years," she stated, "the oldest written Constitution still in force in the world." To serve on this court, she continued, "is the highest honor, the most awesome trust that can be placed in a judge. It means working at my craft—working with and for the law—as a way to keep our society both ordered and free."[4]

Ginsburg also let the senators know that as a judge she needed to maintain "impartiality" on matters that might later come before the court. In what would become known as the "Ginsburg Precedent," she declared that she would not be able to answer questions as to how she would rule on a particular issue. "Because I am and hope to continue to be a judge," she remarked, "it would be wrong for me to say or preview in this legislative chamber how I would cast my vote on questions the Supreme Court may be called upon to decide. Were I to rehearse here what I would say and how I would reason on such questions, I would act injudiciously."[5]

Following her statement, committee members began peppering Ginsburg with questions on everything from abortion and the death penalty to discrimination and gay rights. On the abortion controversy, Ginsburg's stance over the years had failed to please both sides of the issue. As a cen-tral figure in the WRP, Ginsburg, most assumed, had to be pro-choice. However, in public comments in the years since *Roe v. Wade* was decided, Ginsburg had expressed some con-cerns about the ruling, among them that the decision ought to have been based on the Fourteenth Amendment's Equal Protection Clause rather than the right to privacy. She also felt that the decision was written too broadly and needlessly

Supreme Court nominee Ruth Bader Ginsburg testifies before the Senate Judiciary Committee on Capitol Hill in Washington, D.C., on July 20, 1993. Ginsburg impressed committee members with stories of how she overcame sexual discrimination through-out her career, while also discussing a range of legal issues.

provoked a backlash. This led many pro-choice activists to wonder whether Ginsburg could be trusted to hold the nar-row pro-choice balance on the Supreme Court.

When asked about abortion, however, Ginsburg ignored her own precedent and placed herself firmly in the pro-choice camp: "This is something central to a woman's life, to her dignity. It's a decision that she must make for herself. And when government controls that decision for her, she's being treated as less than a fully adult human responsible for her own choices."[6]

On the death penalty, Senator Orrin Hatch and Senator Arlen Specter, the latter a Republican representing Pennsylvania, sought to pin down Ginsburg on the matter, asking whether she felt it was constitutional or, more broadly, what her personal opinion was on the issue. Ginsburg repeatedly fended off their questions, telling them that as a judge, it would be unwise for her to forecast a future opinion.

Ginsburg also offered a lengthy analysis of the Fourteenth Amendment, which granted equal protection under the law and was the basis for many of her legal challenges on behalf of the WRP. "It is part of our history—a sad part of our history, Senator Specter, but undeniably part of our history—that the 14th Amendment, that great amendment that changed so much in this nation, was not intended by its framers immediately to change the status of women,"[7] she said. As a consequence, Ginsburg remarked:

> I remain an advocate of the Equal Rights Amendment for this reason: because I have a daughter and a granddaughter. . . . I would like the legislators of this country and of all the states to stand up and say we know what that history was in the 19th century; we want to make a clarion announcement that women and men are equal before the law.[8]

Senator Edward "Ted" Kennedy of Massachusetts asked Ginsburg to discuss how she felt about discrimination. In an eloquent reply, Ginsburg stated:

Senator Kennedy, I am alert to discrimination. I grew up during World War II in a Jewish family. I have memories as a child, even before the war, of being in a car with my parents and passing a place in [Pennsylvania], a resort with a sign out in front that read: "No dogs or Jews allowed." Signs of that kind existed in this country during my childhood. One couldn't help but be sensitive to discrimination living as a Jew in America at the time of World War II.[9]

However, when pressed on how she would rule on matters relating to discrimination based on sexual orientation, Ginsburg again refused to preview her decision.

In a more personal question, Senator Herb Kohl, a Wisconsin Democrat, asked how she would like to be viewed by others. Ginsburg responded, "As someone who

THE EQUAL RIGHTS AMENDMENT

First proposed in the 1920s, the Equal Rights Amendment (ERA) sought to enshrine gender equality into the Constitution. While the amendment's initial prospects were not very bright, by the early 1970s, both houses of Congress had approved it by two-thirds majority. The amendment decreed, "Equality of rights under the law shall not be denied or abridged by the United States or any State on account of sex." According to the Constitution, any proposed amendment to the supreme law of the United States needed to be approved by three-quarters of the state legislatures. Unfortunately for ERA backers, by the June 1982 deadline, only 35 of the required 38 states had approved the amendment, and it failed to pass.

cares about people and does the best she can with the talent she has to make a contribution to a better world."[10]

After three days of open testimony and a daylong, closed-door session with members of the judiciary committee, Ginsburg's confirmation hearings came to a close. Everyone agreed that she had performed admirably, though some were frustrated with her reticence. For his part, President Clinton offered high praise for his nominee's conduct. Ginsburg had shown, in the president's words, "tremendous intellect, integrity, comprehension of the law and compassion for the concerns of all Americans."[11]

In conjunction with her public testimony, Ginsburg also had to submit to a thorough examination of her family's financial records. Given the Ginsburgs' fastidious record keeping—Martin was a tax attorney, after all—no red flags came up. In fact, it turned out that Martin was the tax attorney of one of President Clinton's opponents in the 1992 election, Texas billionaire H. Ross Perot. The examination disclosed that the Ginsburgs had a net worth of $6.1 million, which would make Ruth the wealthiest justice, pending her confirmation.

A NEW JUSTICE

Following the conclusion of their examination, the Senate Judiciary Committee, in a unanimous 18–0 vote, recommended that Ginsburg's nomination be brought before the whole Senate for confirmation. Then, on August 3, 1993, the Senate, in a near-unanimous vote of 96–3, confirmed Ginsburg's nomination. A week later, on August 10, Chief Justice William Rehnquist administered the oath of office, and Ruth Bader Ginsburg became the one hundred-seventh justice of the United States Supreme Court. She was the second woman ever named to the court (the first being Sandra Day O'Connor, nominated by President Reagan in 1981) and the first woman of Jewish heritage.

Ruth Bader Ginsburg takes the oath of office from Chief Justice William Rehnquist *(right)* during a ceremony in the East Room of the White House in Washington, D.C., on August 10, 1993. Ginsburg's husband Martin holds the Bible as President Bill Clinton looks on at left.

Since her days growing up on the streets of Brooklyn, breathing in the smell of Chinese food as she read in the library with her mother, Ginsburg had striven with single-minded dedication to reach this point. Sexism, cancer in the family, the demands of motherhood—all could have led her to change course and follow a less ambitious path. But in the end, her talent and perseverance helped her reach the pinnacle of her profession, trading in her seat on the appeals court for the robes of a Supreme Court justice.

Her First Days
on the Bench

Having taken the oath as a Supreme Court justice, Ruth Bader Ginsburg prepared for her debut on the Court. Supreme Court sessions begin on the first Monday in October and end in late June or early July. During that time, there is an awful lot of work to get through. When Ginsburg first joined the Court in 1993, the justices and their staffs received more than 7,000 petitions each year from litigants who believed their cases should be heard by the Court. Of those 7,000, the Supreme Court selected between about 65 and 130 to rule on.

Ginsburg's first task was to move into her new chambers at the Supreme Court, located across the street from the U.S. Capitol. Ginsburg selected Thurgood Marshall's former offices on the second floor, a fitting choice for the woman dubbed the "Thurgood Marshall of the Women's Movement." In decorating her five-room office suite, which overlooks a pleasant courtyard, Ginsburg chose to go with a more modern look rather than the antique style of leather and oak favored by most of the other justices. She also hired her staff, which consisted of four law clerks, two secretaries, and a chamber's aide or messenger. For the first time ever on the Court, Ginsburg permitted one of her clerks to have flexible hours so that he could help care for his young child while his wife worked.

In her first official day on the Court, October 1, 1993, Ginsburg was welcomed into the Supreme Court family with an official ceremony, photography session, and dinner party. Two people in particular were especially happy to see her on the Court. One was Justice Sandra Day O'Connor. As the only woman on the Court for 12 years, O'Connor had endured a number of indignities: for example, there was no bathroom for women justices until Ginsburg's arrival. Prior to that, O'Connor shared a bathroom used by the chief justice's secretaries. Out in public, many assumed her husband was the Supreme Court justice. "That happened many times," O'Connor remarked. "People would come up and say how wonderful it was to meet a justice, and they'd shake John's hand. He'd laugh. He has a good sense of humor."[1] So when she first met her new colleague, O'Connor greeted her with a heartfelt hug. "It made a huge difference when Justice Ginsburg came on [to the Court]. I was so glad to have company," she later recalled. "Immediately, the media started treating us like fungible justices, not so much focused on a single woman. It made an immediate big difference."[2]

In addition to Justice O'Connor, there was another justice who was happy to see Ginsburg arrive on the Supreme Court for her company, if not for her judicial philosophy: her good friend Antonin Scalia, who had served with

Justice Ruth Bader Ginsburg *(center)* poses with her family at the Supreme Court in Washington, D.C., on October 1, 1993. From left are her son-in-law, George Spera Jr.; her daughter, Jane; her husband, Martin; and her son, James. The justice's grandchildren, Clara and Paul Spera, are in front.

Ginsburg on the Court of Appeals for the D.C. Circuit before becoming a Supreme Court justice himself in 1986.

THE JUNIOR JUSTICE

For her first year on the Court, before the confirmation of Justice Stephen Breyer in 1994, Ginsburg was the junior justice. It is the junior justice's responsibility to, among other obligations, serve as the secretary and doorkeeper of the justices' private conferences, taking notes, keeping tallies of the votes on what cases to hear, answering the door if anyone knocks, and reporting developments to the court clerk.

It is common for new justices to feel overwhelmed with their new responsibilities. Ruth Bader Ginsburg was no

DID YOU KNOW?

A Profound Friendship

While serving together on the D.C. Circuit, Ruth Bader Ginsburg and Antonin Scalia struck up a deep and some would say unlikely friendship. Among the most conservative judges when on the D.C. Circuit and currently on the Supreme Court, Scalia has rarely been on the same page as Ginsburg in interpreting the U.S. Constitution. Their styles are vastly different as well: Scalia is as well known for his confrontational approach in both his written legal opinions and in his questioning of attorneys appearing before the Supreme Court as Ginsburg is for her reserve and tact. Yet both judges had much in common: In addition to their love for the law, they both were opera buffs and each had spent their childhoods in New York City. The Scalias and Ginsburgs on occasion spent vacations and New Year's Eves with one another. During her early tenure on the court, Ginsburg traveled with Scalia to India to discuss legal issues with Indian judges and attorneys. During their stay, they traveled to Jaipur, where they rode an elephant, a picture of which hangs in Ginsburg's Supreme Court office. In January 1994, Ginsburg and Scalia exchanged their judicial robes for powdered wigs and seventeenth-century costumes, appearing as extras onstage at a production of the Washington Opera.

exception. With more than 1,500 petitions to review, she had an enormous amount of material to sift through. In her first several months on the Court, she recalled, "I found myself chained to my desk."[3] Much of her time was spent reviewing death penalty cases. "I had no idea how many hours the Justices spend dealing with death cases," she stated. "Every capital case is on the discuss list, and each Justice's chambers is alert for each pre-execution vigil."[4] As in the past, when

Justices Ruth Bader Ginsburg and Antonin Scalia (*center*) pose with the cast of *Ariadne auf Naxos* following a performance at the Washington Opera on January 8, 1994. (The justices appeared as extras during the performance.) Although opposites in judicial philosophy, the justices are very close friends and fellow opera lovers.

shouldered with an extra heavy workload, Ginsburg some-how found the time to attend to all her duties. During her first several months on the Supreme Court, she was observed going through legal briefs while out to dinner at a restaurant with her husband. At a movie theater, she was seen reading court papers by flashlight during the previews.

Undaunted by her responsibilities, Ginsburg made her presence felt early on. In the majority of cases that come before the court, each side is given a half hour to present its arguments. During that time, justices may pose questions to the counselors. Some justices, like Antonin Scalia, ask a number of questions to find inconsistencies in the attor-neys' reasoning. Other justices, such as Clarence Thomas, for example, stay largely silent. On her first day on the bench, Ginsburg and her eight colleagues all shook hands according to custom and then took their seats. As the junior justice, Ginsburg took her place at the far left of the nine, with Chief Justice William Rehnquist occupying the middle seat. During the first hour of arguments, in her first session as a justice, Ginsburg asked 17 questions, giving notice that she would not be a novice observer but rather an engaged participant in the proceedings, even though she was new to the bench. While some felt she posed too many questions, others offered a ringing endorsement. "Making the most impressive high-court debut in memory, Justice Ruth Bader Ginsburg gave a clinic on how to hit the ground running," one writer noted. "Ginsburg provided a strong reminder of what happens when a president sends an extremely well-qualified candidate to the bench."[5]

"JUST DO IT"

Whenever Ginsburg needed advice, she often went to Justice O'Connor—whom she described as "like a big sister"[6]—during her early years on the Court. In her first days on the bench, Ginsburg found herself with a problem.

Members of the U.S. Supreme Court prepare to pose for their official group portrait in Washington, D.C., on December 3, 1993, during Ruth Bader Ginsburg's first year in office. Standing from left are Clarence Thomas, Anthony M. Kennedy, David Souter, and Ginsburg. Seated from left are Sandra Day O'Connor, Harry Blackmun, Chief Justice William Rehnquist, John Paul Stevens, and Antonin Scalia.

The chief justice, who determines which justice will write a particular opinion, had given Ginsburg a rather difficult case. Customarily, the new justice's first opinion assignment is an easy one, not especially complex and likely to generate a near-unanimous consensus among her colleagues. Ginsburg's first assignment, however, concerned a complicated law dealing with benefits for federal workers on which the justices were closely divided. Not sure how to proceed, Ginsburg turned to O'Connor for counsel. "Just do it," O'Connor encouraged her. "And if you can, get your draft in circulation before the next set of assignments is made."[7] O'Connor's advice was sound: rather than worry about the best approach, how to build consensus, the most important thing was to do the job and write the opinion. Though

SANDRA DAY O'CONNOR

A true trailblazer, Sandra Day O'Connor was born in El Paso, Texas, on March 26, 1930, to Harry Aldred Day and the former Ada Mae Wilkey. Because the Days were a cattle-ranching family, Sandra grew up on the Lazy B, a secluded ranch in southeastern Arizona. Her childhood lacked many of the comforts of modern living. For the first years of her life, there was no electricity or running water on the ranch. Nor were there any other children to play with. The young Sandra found companionship with the older ranch hands and with animals. For her education, she was sent to live with her grandparents in El Paso, where she attended the Radford School, graduating at the age of 16. She went on to college at Stanford University, graduating magna cum laude in 1950 with a degree in economics. She then entered Stanford Law School, where she served on the law review and met her future husband, John Jay O'Connor. She needed only two years to complete her degree, graduating third in a class of 102. The future Supreme Court chief justice, William Rehnquist, was ranked first.

Despite her impressive achievements, no law firm in California would offer her a position, so she took up a post as deputy county attorney for San Mateo. After John was drafted into the army, the O'Connors spent several years in Germany before settling in Phoenix, Arizona. Unfortunately, job prospects for a female attorney had not improved while

O'Connor ultimately dissented on Ginsburg's first ruling, she included a note for Ginsburg that read, "This is your first opinion for the Court. It is a fine one. I look forward to many more."[8]

the O'Connors were overseas, so Sandra opened her own law firm. While taking time off to raise her three sons, Sandra got involved with charity work and the Republican Party. She became an assistant state attorney general and was later appointed to a vacant seat in the state senate. Elected twice in her own right, she was voted majority leader of the state senate by her colleagues, the first woman in the country ever so honored. In 1974, she was elected to the Maricopa County Superior Court. In 1979, the governor appointed her to the Arizona Court of Appeals. Two years later, with the retirement of Justice Potter Stewart, President Ronald Reagan nominated her to the Supreme Court. On September 21, 1981, the Senate voted 99–0 to confirm her.

As the first female justice on the Supreme Court, O'Connor charted her own path. Though she tended to side with the conservatives, especially in her early tenure, she later earned a reputation as a frequent swing vote, a centrist who sought to build consensus and help moderate a Court that had grown increasingly divided over the years. With her husband stricken with Alzheimer's disease, O'Connor was forced to retire from the bench and stepped down on January 31, 2006. In recognition of her contributions to the nation, President Barack Obama awarded her the country's highest civilian honor, the Presidential Medal of Freedom, on August 21, 2009.

Ginsburg's first year on the Court was an eventful one: A large percentage of the cases during the 1993–1994 term dealt with sexual harassment and other forms of gender discrimination. Other cases involved abortion rights, freedom of speech, and affirmative action. In total, the Supreme Court ruled on 82 cases that term, its lowest total in nearly 40 years.

Unfortunately, those who had hoped that Ginsburg would help build consensus on a divided court were soon disappointed. Though she had shown success in this regard on the Court of Appeals, not even Ginsburg's talent and energy could bridge the often-wide ideological differences that existed among the justices. Much of this could be chalked up to numbers. On the appeals court, only three judges rule on a particular case, while all nine justices have their say in Supreme Court decisions. "I can appreciate why unanimity is so much harder to achieve in Supreme Court judgments," a philosophical Ginsburg commented. "It is ever so much easier to have a conversation among three than nine."[9]

In her early years on the Court, Ginsburg developed a reputation as a liberal justice in most areas of the law, with the exception of criminal cases, where she frequently sided with her more conservative counterparts. Still, her rulings tended to rely on an incremental, procedural approach, rather than a more sweeping and ambitious one. However, one recurring problem for the new justice was being confused with her colleague, Justice O'Connor. The two bore no resemblance to each other, yet they were repeatedly mixed up. The problem was not entirely unexpected. Early on in Ginsburg's tenure, the National Association of Women Judges had presented both her and O'Connor with T-shirts. Ginsburg's read "I'm Ruth, not Sandra," while O'Connor's stated, "I'm Sandra, not Ruth." A frustrated Ginsburg wrote in 1997, "Just last term our Acting Solicitor

General three times called me Justice O'Connor, and the same slip was made by a distinguished advocate, Harvard Law School Professor Lawrence Tribe."[10]

THE GINSBURG FAMILY GROWS (AGAIN)

As a judge, Ginsburg has the power to perform marriages. During her time on the Supreme Court, she has presided over the marriages of many family members and friends. No doubt the most meaningful of these ceremonies was the one that took place on November 17, 1995, when she married her son, James, to Lisa Brauston, an art historian. As she opened the proceedings, the mother of the groom stated:

> When James and Lisa asked me to officiate at this wedding ceremony, I was at once pleased and concerned—pleased that they would want me to preside as we witness their declarations and exchange of vows; concerned that I could manage my part with no tears. But if there are tears, James and Lisa, they will be for your happiness.[11]

In her touching speech, she spoke of how Lisa had impacted her son's life for the better, remarking, "Since Lisa came into [his] life, he has seemed more satisfied with himself, more content with his work and days, more eager to pursue the joy and music of being alive."[12]

Three years after they were married, on April 30, 1998, James and Lisa added another member to the Ginsburg family, a daughter, Miranda Erin Ginsburg. Ginsburg's three grandchildren all refer to her as "Bubbe," the Yiddish word for grandmother.

UNITED STATES V. VIRGINIA

Given her work for the WRP, perhaps no decision gave Ginsburg more satisfaction than the one she wrote in

United States v. Virginia in 1996. In this case, the admission policy of the Virginia Military Institute (VMI), a state-run facility, was called into question. Since its establishment in 1839, VMI had admitted men only. Lower courts had ruled that this policy violated the Equal Protection Clause of the Fourteenth Amendment and needed to be remedied. In response, Virginia proposed to establish the Virginia Women's Institute for Leadership (VWIL), an all-female facility, while maintaining VMI's male-only admission policy. Writing for a 7–1 majority, Ginsburg ruled that the separate facility would not do and that VMI must admit women:

> The United States maintains that the Constitution's equal protection guarantee precludes Virginia from reserving exclusively to men the unique education opportunities VMI affords. We agree. . . . To cure that violation, and to afford genuinely equal protection, women seeking and fit for a VMI-quality education cannot be offered anything less.[13]

With the VMI admission policy, Ginsburg argued, Virginia "serves the state's sons, [but] makes no provision whatever for her daughters. That is not equal protection. . . . There is no reason to believe that the admission of women capable of all the activities required of VMI cadets would destroy the Institute rather than enhance its capacity to serve 'the more perfect Union.'"[14] Shortly after rendering this decision, on January 20, 1997, Ginsburg had the honor of administering the oath of office to Vice President Al Gore at Bill Clinton's second inaugural.

BATTLING CANCER

Throughout her time on the Court, Ginsburg has traveled widely, delivering lectures and teaching classes at various educational institutions throughout the world, from Great

Britain, Spain, and France to Israel, India, and Austria. The summer of 1999 found her teaching with Martin on the Mediterranean island of Crete. While there, Ruth experienced a sharp pain in her abdomen. Doctors eventually attributed her discomfort to a stomach infection. In the course of their examination, however, the doctors found cancer in Ginsburg's colon. Luckily, they were able to catch it early, thanks to the well-timed but unrelated stomach infection. Ginsburg entered Washington Hospital Center, where doctors removed her sigmoid colon—a two-foot-long section on the lower portion of the large intestine—and a small malignant tumor. After 11 days, she was released and returned home to recuperate. Ginsburg was "very lucky to have had this picked up incidentally," Dr. Harmon Erye of the American Cancer Society remarked. "If it had been left alone it would have advanced to another stage."[15]

Though the recuperation for such procedures is expected to take at least a month, Ruth returned to work barely a week after getting out of the hospital. On October 5, 1999, the Supreme Court opened its session with Ruth Bader Ginsburg in her customary seat. Throughout her career, she had demonstrated that nothing could stop her from fulfilling her goals—not the loss of her mother, not discrimination nor the demands of motherhood, and certainly not cancer.

Bush v. Gore and the War on Terror

Throughout the 200-plus years of its existence, the U.S. Supreme Court has made history on a fairly regular basis. Yet, even for a body accustomed to interpreting the nation's laws and helping set its future, nothing could have prepared the justices for what they were called upon to do in the case of *Bush v. Gore*. For Justice Ruth Bader Ginsburg and her colleagues, the experience was a difficult one, and the results influenced the direction of the Court for years to come.

The election of 2000 pitted Vice President Al Gore against Governor George W. Bush of Texas. The polls leading up to Election Day showed a remarkably close race. On Tuesday, November 7, Americans across the country cast their ballots. As the results trickled in, the election proved even closer than anticipated—and it all came down to Florida. Without Florida's electoral votes, neither candidate could claim the 270 votes in the Electoral College necessary to win the presidency. On election night, the television networks first called the state for Gore, then for Bush, before ending the night with the declaration that Florida was "too close to call." The next day, out of the nearly 6 million votes cast, Bush, the Republican candidate, was found to have a lead of just 1,784 votes. The close margin required every county to conduct an automatic machine recount. This cut Bush's lead to 327. Given the razor-thin margin, more recounts were inevitable.

As the nation's eyes turned to the Sunshine State, the Gore campaign requested manual recounts in four counties that had large numbers of so-called "undervotes"—ballots that did not register a preference for either presidential candidate in the machine count but might indicate one on closer examination. These counties were also heavily Democratic, so it was more likely that uncounted ballots would favor the vice president. In response, on November 11, the Bush team filed a lawsuit in federal court seeking to halt the recount, declaring that the "selective" recounts (recounts being made in only heavily Democratic counties) violated the Equal Protection Clause of the Fourteenth Amendment. Judge Donald M. Middlebrooks rejected the challenge, permitting the recounts to continue, declaring that the state had the responsibility to determine how it selects its presidential electors and that, up until this preliminary point in the process, the recount seemed to be neutral, favoring neither side in the dispute.

As the recounts progressed, it became clear that they would take longer than a week. Yet, according to Florida state law, the secretary of the state of Florida, Katherine Harris, a Republican, should certify the election results by the seventh day. It also allowed the secretary to extend the deadline. Though only one of the four counties had completed their recounts, Harris moved to certify the results on the seventh day and declare Bush the winner. However, the Florida Supreme Court intervened, ruling that the secretary of state must not certify the election results until November 26, thus giving the recount five more days to proceed. In response, the Bush team appealed to the U.S. Supreme Court on a number of grounds. On November 24, needing only four votes to hear the case of *Bush v. Palm Beach County Canvassing Board*, the U.S. Supreme Court ruled five to four to hear it. Justice Ginsburg was among the four who voted against.

As this struggle played out in the courts, other events were occurring on the ground. The national tally of votes showed the vice president with a narrow lead in the popular vote. (It is possible for a candidate to be ahead in the popular vote and still not achieve a majority of votes in the Electoral College. The presidential elections of 1876, 1888, and, as we shall see, 2000, produced an Electoral College winner who did not win a majority of the nationwide popular vote.) Meanwhile, in Miami-Dade, one of the counties in which Gore had requested a recount, Bush supporters had disrupted and shut down the work of the canvassing board. Then, on November 26, though only two of the four counties had completed their recounts, Katherine Harris certified the results, declaring Bush the winner. The Gore team in turn filed a "contest," noting its intention to dispute the election results.

Meanwhile, on December 4, the U.S. Supreme Court released a *per curiam* or "by the court"[1] decision in the *Bush v. Palm Beach County Canvassing Board* case. Rather than overturning the lower court's ruling, the Court vacated it, declaring that the Florida Supreme Court had not explained itself well enough. However, since Harris had

Counters and observers conduct a hand recount of Broward County ballots at the Broward Emergency Operation Center in Plantation, Florida, on
November 19, 2000, following the disputed presidential election. The U.S.
Supreme Court would ultimately help to decide the winner of the 2000
presidential election.

already followed the ruling, not declaring Bush the winner
until November 26, as the court had ruled, the point was
largely moot. This was not, however, to be the Supreme
Court's last decision on the 2000 election.

The same day of the *Bush v. Palm Beach County Canvassing
Board* decision, Judge N. Sanders Saul of the Leon County
Circuit Court, ruled against Gore's contest motion in the
case of *Gore v. Harris*. The Gore team appealed the decision
to the Florida Supreme Court. On December 8, the Florida
Supreme Court overruled Judge Saul and ordered a manual
recount of all undervotes in all Florida counties. At this
point, after the two completed recounts and two aborted
ones, Bush was leading Gore by either just 154 or 193 votes

statewide. With 60,000 undervotes to be sifted through, the election appeared far from over.

As the recount process got under way, lawyers for the Bush team were crafting their appeal to the Supreme Court. Three of the more conservative justices on the Court, Antonin Scalia, Clarence Thomas, and Chief Justice Rehnquist, all wanted to overturn the lower court's ruling without hearing legal arguments, a sign of their deep disagreement with the Florida Supreme Court's actions. Justices Anthony Kennedy and Sandra Day O'Connor, however, were prepared to hear the litigants, while Ginsburg and fellow justices David Souter, Stephen Breyer, and John Paul Stevens did not feel the decision needed to be reviewed. The united front that the Court had displayed in the Palm Beach County case quickly collapsed. The Supreme Court would hear the case on December 11.

After lawyers for the two candidates presented their arguments, the justices returned to their chambers to consider how they would rule. The liberal justices, Ginsburg among them, felt the recount should continue. Of these, Breyer and Souter thought that a uniform standard ought to be developed for counting the ballots one way or the other. On the other side, Rehnquist, Thomas, Scalia, and O'Connor felt the lower court had overstepped its bounds and that its ruling ought to be overturned and the recount halted. The deciding vote came down to Justice Kennedy.

Kennedy sided with the conservatives. He believed that the recount should be halted, citing the Equal Protection Clause as the basis for his decision. Whatever procedures were put in place, he felt, could not guarantee equal protection, and he argued that the different standards for counting ballots would make one vote more important than another. As the various drafts of the justices' rulings were circulated, Ginsburg was angered by Kennedy's reliance on the Equal Protection Clause. She had built her career with the WRP on using the Equal Protection Clause to eliminate discrimination; here she felt it was being employed to discount votes. Initially, she inserted a footnote in her dissent referring to press reports that suggested that in Florida the African-American vote, a firmly Democratic constituency, had been suppressed by local and state authorities, implying that if equal protection was a concern, there were other aspects of the election that ought to be considered. After an angry exchange with Scalia, she removed the reference.

On December 12, 2000, the disputed election finally came to an end. Ruling 5–4 in the case of *Bush v. Gore*, the U.S. Supreme Court halted the recount and upheld the

IN HER OWN WORDS

Registering her disagreement with her colleagues in the case of *Bush v. Gore*, which helped decide the 2000 presidential election, Justice Ruth Bader Ginsburg issued a powerful dissenting opinion:

> In sum, the Court's conclusion that a constitutionally adequate recount is impractical is a prophecy the Court's own judgment will not allow to be tested. Such an untested prophecy should not decide the Presidency of the United States. I dissent.*

*Steve Cobble, "Supreme Injustice," *The Nation.* June 23, 2001, http://www.thenation.com/doc/20010709/cobble20010623.

certification of George W. Bush as the winner of Florida's decisive electoral votes. With these votes, the Texas governor won the presidency. The ruling, mostly written by Kennedy, was roundly criticized in its reasoning if not in its outcome. Kennedy held that the ruling only applied to this one case and thus was not the basis for any legal precedent—a rather unusual statement for any judge, let alone one on the Supreme Court, to make. Ginsburg, Stevens, Breyer, and Souter issued firm dissents.

The long election ordeal now over, the justices sought a return to normalcy. Despite their disagreements in *Bush v. Gore*, Ginsburg and Scalia spent New Year's Eve together along with their families. In order to continue their work, the justices had to lay to rest the divisions that had erupted during the tumultuous election dispute. "We had to go on and do the work of the court and we did," Ginsburg stated. "And if you were going to bear grudges, that would not be possible. It's almost like a trust that we are bound to preserve the institution and give it to our successors in the same good condition that we received it."[2]

THE WAR ON TERROR

Following the September 11, 2001, terror attacks on the United States, which killed almost 3,000 people at the World Trade Center in New York City, at the Pentagon outside Washington, D.C., and in Pennsylvania, the Bush administration claimed extensive powers to combat terrorists associated with the al-Qaeda network. Many legal issues arising from what was coming to be called the "War on Terror" came up for review before the Supreme Court. Of particular interest were the rights of detainees—those suspected of posing a terrorist threat but who had not yet been charged with any crimes. The Bush administration claimed the power to detain suspected terrorists, whether they were U.S. citizens or foreign nationals.

Three such terrorism cases worked their way through the lower courts, arriving before Ginsburg and her fellow justices in 2004. The *Hamdi v. Rumsfeld* case arose after an American citizen named Yasir Hamdi, who was captured in Afghanistan in 2001 by U.S.-backed Afghan forces while he was fighting al-Qaeda and their associates in the Taliban. Suspecting Hamdi of being a Taliban guerrilla, the U.S. government declared him an "enemy combatant" and held him without charge, shipping him first to Guantanamo Bay, Cuba, and then to a military prison in Virginia for an indefinite stay. Hamdi's father sued, accusing the government of violating his son's due process rights by failing to charge him or allow him legal counsel. On April 28, 2004, the Supreme Court ruled 8–1, with Justice Thomas the lone dissenter, that Hamdi's rights had been violated. Writing for the plurality, however, Justice O'Connor declared that an act of Congress had authorized the administration to detain those, like Hamdi, that it claimed were enemy combatants, but that the government had violated his right of due process by not offering him a legal hearing to challenge his imprisonment. In a concurring opinion, Justice Souter, joined by Ginsburg, held that they did not believe Congress authorized the indefinite imprisonment of enemy combatants.

The same day as the *Hamdi* ruling, the Court announced its decision in *Rumsfeld v. Padilla*. Returning from a trip to Pakistan, José Padilla, an American citizen, was detained at O'Hare Airport in Chicago, first as a witness in a terrorism case and then because he was suspected of plotting terrorist attacks on American soil. As it had with Hamdi, the U.S. government declared Padilla an enemy combatant, held him without charge, and denied him the advice of an attorney. Lower courts had ruled that Padilla's rights as a citizen had been violated. The government appealed to the Supreme Court. The question before the justices was whether Congress had authorized such measures and whether those measures were constitutional. In the Court's 5–4 decision, however, Chief Justice Rehnquist, joined by O'Connor, Thomas, Scalia, and Kennedy, did not rule on the merits of the case; rather, he declared that the case had been filed in the wrong jurisdiction and against the wrong person. Padilla's lawyer, who filed the complaint in federal court in New York, was not informed that his client had been transferred to South Carolina, and the commander of the facility where Padilla was held, rather than Donald Rumsfeld, the secretary of defense, should have been the target of the suit. Justices Stevens, Ginsburg, Souter, and Breyer disagreed. Given the circumstances, they argued, an exception should have been made and the constitutional questions raised should have been decided. Breyer felt the majority's decision once again kept Padilla from a fair hearing and constituted a grave threat to American liberty. Ginsburg herself drew attention for her pointed questioning of the government's attorney.

(Amid the deliberations on the enormous constitutional questions that the Court was trying to answer, Ginsburg took time for a personal milestone. On June 23, 2004, she and Martin celebrated their fiftieth wedding anniversary. "In love," Ginsburg has quipped, "I was lucky."[3])

In *Rasul v. Bush*, which was decided on June 28, 2004, Ginsburg signed on to a 6–3 ruling authored by Justice Stevens. In this case, several Australian and British citizens were captured in Afghanistan, declared enemy combatants by the U.S. government, and held without charge and without access to attorneys in Guantanamo Bay. The Bush administration argued that since they were enemy combatants and not American citizens and were not held on American soil, they had no standing to challenge their imprisonment. Lower courts concurred with the administration, but the Supreme Court did not. With Justices Scalia,

Thomas, and Rehnquist dissenting, the majority opinion declared that the detainees had the right to a hearing to challenge their detention and that the administration's legal reasoning was faulty.

Taken together, these three decisions, *Rasul* and *Hamdi* especially, reined in some of the powers the Bush administration had sought in waging the War on Terror. By her votes in these cases, Ginsburg had shown her discomfort with the claims made by the executive branch. As the 2003–2004 term came to a close, another national election was on the horizon, one that would have a lasting effect on the Supreme Court.

Standing
Her Ground

Following President George W. Bush's narrow reelection victory over Senator John Kerry of Massachusetts in November 2004, few had any doubts that the president would soon have the opportunity to name at least one new justice to the Supreme Court. Although more than 70 years old, Ruth Bader Ginsburg had no plans to retire, despite having served on the court for more than a decade. Her colleagues on the bench, however, were another story.

DEATH THREATS

But before any roster changes occurred, the Supreme Court weighed in on the complex case of Terri Schiavo in early 2005. Doctors had diagnosed Schiavo as being in a persistent vegetative state since lapsing into a coma in February

1990, and she had been kept alive through feeding tubes for the past 15 years. Based on conversations he had with her before her illness, her husband, Michael, believed that she would not want to remain on life support. Eventually, he received a Florida court order allowing that her feeding tube be removed so she could be allowed to die. Terri's parents, Robert and Mary Schindler, however, wanted her to be kept alive. The Supreme Court had refused to hear an appeal of the lower court's decision several times. Having failed to move the courts, the Schindlers went to Congress, enlisting the aid of the Republican majority and President Bush. Congress passed and the president signed a bill stating that the federal court in Florida had to hold a hearing to determine whether the feeding tube should be removed. At this hearing, the judge again rejected the Schindlers' petition. Once more, the Schindlers appealed to the Supreme Court. On March 24, the Supreme Court refused to hear the case, the feeding tubes were removed, and Schiavo died on March 31, 2005.

Following Schiavo's death, Republicans in Congress vented their anger at the courts. The majority leader of the House of Representatives, Tom DeLay, threatened to impeach the judges involved in rejecting the Schindlers' appeals. "The time will come for the men responsible for this to answer for their behavior," DeLay commented. "We will look at an arrogant, out-of-control judiciary that thumbs its nose at Congress and the president."[1] Senator John Cornyn of Texas took a similar stance several days later when he made a connection between the Schiavo case and the recent murder of a federal judge's family and the mass murder of a judge and two attendants in an Atlanta, Georgia, courtroom. "I don't know if there is a cause-and-effect connection but we have seen some recent episodes of courthouse violence in this country," he said.

> I wonder whether there may be some connection between the perception in some quarters on some occasions where judges are making political decisions yet are unaccountable to the public, that it builds up and builds up and builds up to the point where some people engage in violence.[2]

On top of Cornyn's remarks, in January 2005 a conservative radio host had jokingly suggested that someone should poison Justice John Paul Stevens.

For O'Connor and Ginsburg, these comments were especially disturbing, since they had both received online death threats around that time. A message in a Web chat room stated, "Okay commandoes, here is your first patriotic assignment . . . an easy one. Supreme Court Justices Ginsburg and O'Connor have publicly stated that they use [foreign] laws and rulings to decide how to rule on American cases. . . . If you are what you say you are, and NOT armchair patriots, then those two justices will not live another week."[3] The next month, the justices were mailed cookies laced with rat poison. While O'Connor spoke out against the venomous rhetoric, Ginsburg remained largely silent, taking the threats in stride and moving ahead with her work.

A NEW COURT TAKES SHAPE

Also in 2005, the Supreme Court underwent some major changes. In the 11 years since Stephen Breyer had joined the bench in 1994, no new justices had been appointed, the same nine judges serving together the entire stretch. Because, however, Chief Justice Rehnquist had been battling cancer for some time, his retirement was anticipated. Despite the chatter, Rehnquist continued to run the Court and made no mention of any plans to step down. O'Connor was also the subject of retirement rumors, given her age and her husband's failing health. On July 5, 2005, O'Connor announced that she would be stepping down. President George W. Bush initially nominated John Glover Roberts Jr., a well-respected conservative judge on the U.S. Court of Appeals for the D.C. Circuit, to succeed her. However, while the country readied for Roberts's confirmation hearing, on September 3, 2005, Chief Justice Rehnquist died. The president subsequently nominated Roberts for chief justice and Harriet Miers, his White House counsel, for O'Connor's seat. The Miers nomination, however, met with resistance from many, including some of the president's own supporters, who believed her to be unqualified, and she subsequently withdrew her name from consideration. The president next selected Samuel Alito Jr., a judge on the U.S. Court of Appeals for the Third Circuit, to succeed O'Connor. After congressional hearings, the Senate confirmed both Roberts and Alito.

With John Roberts succeeding William Rehnquist as chief justice, the balance between the liberal and conservative wings of the Court remained relatively unchanged. Roberts, like his predecessor Rehnquist, was considered a right-of-center judge. In fact, many placed Roberts slightly further to the right of Rehnquist on the spectrum. Rehnquist's conservatism, some contended, had lessened somewhat in his later years, as the Court was remade in his image. Once the lone conservative voice on a liberal bench in his early days as a justice, Rehnquist had seen his conservative views over time become the dominant force on the Court. His work largely completed, the thinking went, he took a more institutionalist approach, working to improve the Supreme Court's operations and focusing more on process. Many saw this change of direction in the opinion Rehnquist wrote in the case of *Dickerson v. United States* in 2000. *Dickerson* upheld the 1966 *Miranda* decision, which decreed that when criminal suspects are

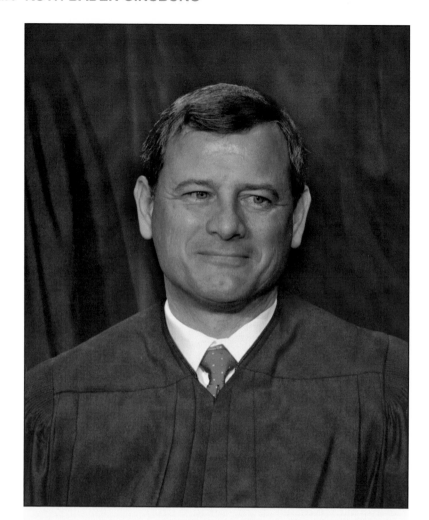

Chief Justice John G. Roberts Jr. at the U.S. Supreme Court in Washington, D.C., on October 31, 2005. His court would prove more conservative in its judicial rulings than the Rehnquist court had been, posing a challenge for the more liberal justices, including Ruth Bader Ginsburg.

arrested, they must be informed of their rights. Earlier in his career, Rehnquist had criticized the *Miranda* ruling. Now, writing for a 7–2 majority, he observed that *Miranda* had become ingrained in American culture and thus should not be overturned. John Roberts, many thought, would not have agreed.

The exchange of Justice O'Connor, a centrist to moderate conservative, however, for Justice Alito, who was ranked among the most conservative jurists in the nation, had a much greater impact on the Court's political balance, tilting it dramatically to the right. As Justice Ginsburg herself observed, "The first full year Justice O'Connor was absent, every 5–4 decision in which I was in dissent, I would have been in the majority had she remained on the Court."[4]

But Ginsburg did not miss only O'Connor's moderating influence on their decisions; she also missed having a fellow woman serving on the bench. Though they often disagreed on the matters before them, she believed as women they both possessed what Ginsburg called "certain sensitivities that our male colleagues lack."[5] The years following O'Connor's retirement were rather lonely ones on the Court for Ginsburg, who was now the sole female justice.

READING FROM THE BENCH

Two Supreme Court rulings in the spring of 2007 were especially troubling for Ginsburg as a women's rights pioneer. The first, *Gonzales v. Carhart*, involved a challenge to the Partial Birth Abortion Ban Act of 2003. This measure, which was passed by Congress and signed by President Bush, banned a particularly controversial late-term abortion procedure. The ban was total. Even if a woman's health, or her life, were at risk, the operation was forbidden. Pro-choice advocates also feared that the law's definition of "partial birth" abortion was vague enough that it might include all late-term abortions. The act was deemed unconstitutional by the lower courts, which based their decisions on earlier Supreme Court rulings on the abortion issue. The Supreme Court, however, by a 5–4 margin, on April 18 overturned the lower courts and upheld the ban. In her dissent, Ginsburg took the unusual step of reading it aloud before the Court:

> In sum, the notion that the Partial-Birth Abortion Ban Act furthers any legitimate governmental interest is, quite simply, irrational. The Court's defense of the statute provides no saving explanation. In candor, the Act, and the Court's defense of it, cannot be understood as anything other than an effort to chip away at a right [to have an abortion] declared again and again by this Court—and with increasing comprehension of its centrality to women's lives.[6]

Late the following month, Ginsburg felt compelled once again to read her dissent from the bench, this time in the case of *Ledbetter v. Goodyear Tire & Rubber Co.* Lilly Ledbetter had retired after working nearly 20 years at a Goodyear tire plant in Alabama. Following her retirement, she discovered that she had been the victim of pay discrimination throughout her career, receiving significantly less salary than her 15 male coworkers with similar positions. Alleging a violation of the 1964 Civil Rights Act, Ledbetter sued Goodyear. A jury agreed with Ledbetter, awarding her $3.5 million, but Goodyear appealed all the way to the Supreme Court. In a strict reading of the 1964 Civil Rights Act, Justice Alito wrote in a 5–4 decision that for Goodyear to be liable for damages, Ledbetter would have had to file her complaint within 180 days of the first act of pay discrimination. Joined by the same justices as in *Gonzales v. Carhart*, Ginsburg issued a stinging dissent, suggesting the majority was ignoring the intent of the Civil Rights Act. She also noted that coworkers rarely know one another's salaries and do not generally ask, making the 180-day window problematic. In a clear and steady voice, Ginsburg stated, "In our view, the court does not comprehend, or is indifferent to, the insidious way in which women can be victims of pay discrimination." The Civil Rights Act, she added, "was meant to govern real-world employment practices, and that world is what the court today ignores."[7] Ginsburg called on Congress to act to correct the injustice. On January 29, 2009, after several false starts by Democrats in Congress during the previous administration, President Obama signed the Lilly Ledbetter Fair Pay Act into law.

IN HER OWN WORDS

Despite the intense differences in judicial philosophy among the justices on the Supreme Court, they remain on good terms with one another, in sharp contrast to the often fractious relations in the U.S. House of Representatives and to a lesser degree in the U.S. Senate, not to mention the many state legislatures and lower courts across the nation. Describing the camaraderie that exists on the Supreme Court, Ruth Bader Ginsburg remarked:

> One thing I should say about the current Court. As different as we are in the way we approach some very hard questions, the Court is a genuinely collegial place. It is more collegial than any law faculty I ever encountered. We genuinely like and care, not just respect, but care about each other. The best example I can give is the year I lived with colorectal cancer. All of my colleagues rallied around me and helped me get through that year without missing a Court sitting.*

* "Conversation Between Justice Ruth Bader Ginsburg & Dean Elena Kagan," *Harvard Journal of Law & Gender*, Summer 2009, p. 243.

Justice Ruth Bader Ginsburg sits with her clerks in her chambers at the Supreme Court in Washington, D.C., on August 7, 2002. Ginsburg's grace and consideration for not only her clerks, but for all of the attorneys who have argued cases before her, is well known and greatly admired.

Reflecting on the purpose of dissents in general, Ginsburg has observed:

> Dissents speak to a future age. It's not simply to say, "My colleagues are wrong and I would do it this way." But the greatest dissents do become court opinions and gradually over time their views become the dominant view. So that's the dissenter's hope: that they are writing not for today but for tomorrow.[8]

JUSTICE SANDRA SOTOMAYOR

With the election of President Barack Obama, a Democrat, in 2008, the rightward drift of the Court was expected to stop. If a vacancy opened up before he left office, Obama would likely fill it with a moderate to liberal justice. The new president did not have to wait long for the opportunity. Justice David Souter announced he would retire on June 29, 2009. Though appointed by a somewhat conservative president, George H.W. Bush, Souter had become a reliable liberal vote on the Court. Throughout his career, Souter displayed a strong independent streak, a common trait in his native New Hampshire, and never took to life in Washington, D.C. Deeply troubled by the *Bush v. Gore* decision, he had contemplated retirement in its aftermath but feared what his departure would mean for the Court. Obama nominated Sandra Sotomayor, a judge on the Court of Appeals for the Second Circuit, to succeed him. She was sworn in on August 6, 2009, becoming the first Hispanic justice and the third woman to sit on the Supreme Court.

Taking advantage of Souter's retirement, Ginsburg traded her chambers for those of the departing justice. After three years on the bench with eight men, Ginsburg welcomed the company of another woman: "I feel great that I don't have to be the lone woman around this place." That experience she compared to "being back in law school in 1956, when there were 9 of us in a class of over 500, so that meant most sections had just 2 women, and you felt that every eye was on you."[9]

ANOTHER BOUT WITH CANCER

During a routine checkup in January 2009, doctors noticed a small, cancerous tumor growing on Ginsburg's pancreas. Pancreatic cancer is one of the most deadly forms of the disease, with only 5 percent of those diagnosed surviving longer than five years. One of the reasons it is so deadly is that symptoms rarely occur before the cancer has spread. Ginsburg's doctors, however, were hopeful that they had caught it early and that her prognosis was not as gloomy as the statistics suggested. In early February, she underwent surgery to have the tumor removed. Barely three weeks later, she was back on the bench. In March, she announced that she would undergo precautionary chemotherapy at the National Institutes of Health. "Thereafter," she stated, "it is anticipated that I will require only routine examinations to assure my continuing good health."[10] In September 2009, however, Ginsburg was admitted to the hospital after feeling faint. She reported her symptoms shortly following an iron glucose injection, which was administered to treat an iron deficiency in her blood, a condition associated with her cancer treatment. She was treated and released the next day.

On June 27, 2010, just four days after he and his wife celebrated their fifty-sixth wedding anniversary, Martin D. Ginsburg passed away from cancer at the family home in Washington, D.C. He was buried in a private ceremony at Arlington National Cemetery. Reflecting on the enduring bond that held the couple together for more than a half century, Martin once observed, "I have been supportive of my wife since the beginning of time, and she has been supportive of me. . . . It's not sacrifice; it's family."[12]

THE FUTURE

Despite her advancing age, Justice Ruth Bader Ginsburg has no plans to retire and has spoken of serving into her eighties. She also is something of a fitness buff, working out with a trainer twice a week to stay in shape. That she would not let cancer slow her down should come as no surprise, given her history. Whatever the future holds, Ginsburg has secured her place in American history, both as a women's rights activist and as a Supreme Court justice. Ginsburg once said, "We should appreciate the women on whose shoulders we stand."[11] Though her final legacy has yet to be written, there can be no doubt that generations of Americans, both men and women, will have cause to appreciate the many achievements of the one hundred-seventh justice of the Supreme Court.

CHRONOLOGY

1933   Ruth Bader is born on March 15 in Brooklyn, New York, to Nathan Bader and the former Celia Amster.

1935   Her older sister, Marilyn, passes away from meningitis.

1946   She graduates from P.S. 238 in Brooklyn on June 24.

1950   Ruth's mother, Celia Bader, dies from cancer at age 47, one day before Ruth graduates from James Madison High School.

1954   She graduates from Cornell University and marries Martin David Ginsburg on June 23.

1955   Ginsburg gives birth to Jane Carol Ginsburg on July 21.

1956   She enters Harvard Law School.

1957   Ginsburg is elected editor of the *Harvard Law Review*.

1958   She transfers to Columbia University Law School.

1959   Ginsburg is elected to *Columbia Law Review* and graduates in a tie for first in her law school class; she begins two-year clerkship with Judge Edmund L. Palmieri on the U.S. District Court for the Southern District of New York.

1961   She travels to Sweden for the first time as part of her research for Columbia's International Procedure Project.

1963   Ginsburg joins the faculty of Rutgers School of Law.

1965   She gives birth to James Steven Ginsburg on September 8; her first book, *Civil Procedure in Sweden*, written with Anders Bruzelius, is published.

1972   She becomes a professor at Columbia University Law School and begins an eight-year stint as co-director of the ACLU's Women's Rights Project.

1973   Ginsburg argues her first case, *Frontiero v. Richardson*, before the Supreme Court on January 17. The Court rules 8–1 in her favor on May 14, 1973; she is named general counsel of the ACLU.

1980   She is nominated by President Jimmy Carter to the U.S. Court of Appeals for the District of Columbia Circuit; she is approved by the Senate and is sworn in on June 30.

1981   Jane Ginsburg marries George Spera Jr.

1986   Her grandson, Paul Bertrand Spera, is born.

1990   Clara Simone Spera, a granddaughter, is born.

1993   Ginsburg is nominated to the Supreme Court by President Bill Clinton on June 13; she is confirmed by the Senate on August 3 and takes the oath of office on August 10.

1995   She officiates at the wedding of her son, James Steven, to Lisa Brauston on November 17.

1997   Ginsburg administers the oath of office to Vice President Al Gore on January 20.

1998   Miranda Erin Ginsburg, a granddaughter, is born on April 30.

1999   Ginsburg is diagnosed with colon cancer; doctors operate to remove the cancer.

2000   On December 4, in the case of *Bush v. Gore*, the Supreme Court rules 5–4 to end the Florida recounts, clearing the way for George W. Bush to become president; Ginsburg dissents.

2004   Martin and Ruth celebrate their fiftieth wedding anniversary on June 23.

2005   Chief Justice William Rehnquist dies on September 5; his successor, John Roberts, is sworn in on September 29.

2009   A cancerous tumor is discovered on Ginsburg's pancreas in January; the following month, she undergoes surgery to remove it; in September, she is hospitalized after feeling faint but is treated and released soon after.

2010   Martin Ginsburg dies on June 27 at age 78 in Washington, D.C. He is buried in Arlington National Cemetery.

NOTES

CHAPTER 1

1. "Clinton Nominates Ginsburg to Supreme Court," *Congressional Quarterly*. June 19, 1993, p. 1,599.
2. Ibid.
3. Henry Reske, "Two Paths for Ginsburg," *ABA Journal*. August 1993, p. 16.
4. "Clinton Nominates Ginsburg to Supreme Court," p. 1,599.
5. "Transcript of President's Announcement and Judge Ginsburg's Remarks," *New York Times*. June 15, 1993. http://www.nytimes.com/1993/06/15/us/supreme-court-transcript-president-s-announcement-judge-ginsburg-s-remarks.html?pagewanted=1.
6. "Clinton Nominates Ginsburg to Supreme Court," p. 1,600.
7. "Transcript of President's Announcement and Judge Ginsburg's Remarks."
8. "Clinton Nominates Ginsburg to Supreme Court," p. 1,600.
9. "Transcript of President's Announcement and Judge Ginsburg's Remarks."
10. Ibid.

CHAPTER 2

1. David Margolick, "Trial by Adversity Shapes Jurist's Outlook," *New York Times*. June 25, 1993, p. A19.
2. Linda Bayer, *Ruth Bader Ginsburg*. Philadelphia: Chelsea House Publishers, 2000, p. 19.
3. Mary Jo Murphy, "Nancy Drew and the Secret of the 3 Black Robes," *New York Times*. May 30, 2009, http://www.nytimes.com/2009/05/31/weekinreview/31murphy.html?_r=3.
4. Bayer, *Ruth Bader Ginsburg*, p. 23.
5. Ibid.

CHAPTER 3

1. Bayer, *Ruth Bader Ginsburg*, pp. 27, 29.
2. Lynn Gilbert and Gaylen Moore, *Particular Passions*. New York: Crown Books, 1981, p. 156.
3. Jeanette Friedman, "Ruth Bader Ginsburg: A Rare Interview," *Lifestyles*. March 1994, p. 12.
4. Stephanie B. Goldberg, "The Second Woman Justice," *ABA Journal*. October 1993, p. 42.
5. Margolick, "Trial by Adversity Shapes Jurist's Outlook."
6. Aaron Epstein and Mary Otto, "Ginsburg Has Pressed for Equality for All," *Sunday Rutland Herald and Sunday Times Argus*. July 4, 1993, p. C4.
7. Bayer, *Ruth Bader Ginsburg*, p. 29.
8. Ibid., p. 30.
9. Ibid., p. 29.
10. Ibid.
11. Margaret Carlson et al, "The Law According to Ruth: Ruth Bader Ginsburg," *Time*. June 28, 1993, p. 38.
12. Bayer, *Ruth Bader Ginsburg*, p. 32.
13. Elinor Porter Swiger, *Women Lawyers at Work*. New York: Julian Messner, 1978, p. 55.
14. Gilbert and Moore, *Particular Passions*, p. 156.
15. Bayer, *Ruth Bader Ginsburg*, p. 38.
16. Gilbert and Moore, *Particular Passions*, p. 158.
17. Bayer, *Ruth Bader Ginsburg*, p. 38.
18. Margolick, "Trial by Adversity Shapes Jurist's Outlook."
19. Bayer, *Ruth Bader Ginsburg*, p. 39.
20. "Justice for Women," *Vogue*. October 1993, p. 473.
21. Margolick, "Trial by Adversity Shapes Jurist's Outlook."
22. Swiger, *Women Lawyers at Work*, p. 55.

CHAPTER 4

1. Swiger, *Women Lawyers at Work*, p. 58.
2. Carlson et al, "The Law According to Ruth," p. 38.
3. Gilbert and Moore, *Particular Passions*, p. 158.
4. Goldberg, "The Second Woman Justice," p. 41.
5. Margolick, "Trial by Adversity Shapes Jurist's Outlook."
6. Gilbert and Moore, *Particular Passions*, p. 158.
7. Ibid.
8. Margolick, "Trial by Adversity Shapes Jurist's Outlook."
9. Bayer, *Ruth Bader Ginsburg*, p. 46.
10. Ibid.
11. Swiger, *Women Lawyers at Work*, p. 62.
12. Bayer, *Ruth Bader Ginsburg*, p. 47.
13. Ibid., p. 48.
14. Gilbert and Moore, *Particular Passions*, p. 159.
15. Bayer, *Ruth Bader Ginsburg*, p. 50.
16. Swiger, *Women Lawyers at Work*, p. 60.
17. Bayer, *Ruth Bader Ginsburg*, p. 50.
18. Swiger, *Women Lawyers at Work*, p. 61.
19. Ibid., p. 69.
20. Bill Hewitt, "Feeling Supreme," *People*. June 28, 1993, p. 50.

CHAPTER 5

1. Gilbert and Moore, *Particular Passions*, p. 153.
2. Oyez Project Web site, http://www.oyez.org/cases/1970-1979/1971/1971_70_4.
3. Ibid.
4. Gilbert and Moore, *Particular Passions*, p. 153.
5. "First No to Sex Bias," *Time*. December 6, 1971, p. 71.

6. Ruth Bader Ginsburg, "Remarks on Women's Progress in the Legal Profession in the United States," *University of Tulsa Law Journal*. 33:13, Fall 1997.

7. Bayer, *Ruth Bader Ginsburg*, p. 56.

8. Ibid., p. 57.

9. Neil A. Lewis, "Woman in the News; Rejected as a Clerk, Chosen as a Justice: Ruth Joan Bader Ginsburg," *New York Times*. June 15, 1993, http://www.nytimes.com/1993/06/15/us/supreme-court-woman-rejected-clerk-chosen-justice-ruth-joan-bader-ginsburg.html?pagewanted=1.

10. Ruth B. Cowan, "Women's Rights Through Litigation," *Columbia Human Rights Law Review*. Spring-Summer 1976, p. 394.

11. Swiger, *Women Lawyers at Work*, p. 52.

12. Epstein and Otto, "Ginsburg Has Pressed for Equality for All," p. C4.

13. "Sex Equality: Impact of a Key Decision," *U.S. News & World Report*. May 28, 1973, p. 69.

14. Cowan, "Women's Rights Through Litigation," p. 394.

15. Bayer, *Ruth Bader Ginsburg*, p. 61.

16. Ibid., p. 53.

17. Swiger, *Women Lawyers at Work*, p. 56.

18. Carmen Bredeson, *Ruth Bader Ginsburg: Supreme Court Justice*. Springfield, N.J.: Enslow Publishers, Inc. 1995, p. 57.

19. Ruth Bader Ginsburg, George Abel Dreyfous Lecture (1978) (on file with the Library of Congress, Ginsburg Collection, Accession 1, Speeches and Writings File, Box 13 at 19).

20. "U.S. Supreme Court: *Califano vs. Goldfarb*," Justia.com, http://supreme.justia.com/us/430/199/case.html.

21. Stephanie B. Goldberg, "Heady ACLU Years," *ABA Journal*. August 1993, p. 18.

CHAPTER 6

1. Steve Komarow, "Ginsburg Says Constitution Will Guide Her," *Rocky Mountain News*. July 21, 1993, p. 2A.
2. Kenneth T. Walsh, "The Elastic Presidency," *U.S. News & World Report*. June 28, 1993, p. 20.
3. David A. Kaplan and Bob Cohn, "A Frankfurter, Not a Hot Dog," *Newsweek*. June 28, 1993, p. 29.
4. Goldberg, "The Second Woman Justice," p. 43.
5. Bayer, *Ruth Bader Ginsburg*, p. 73.
6. Carlson, "The Law According to Ruth," p. 40.
7. *Almanac of the Federal Judiciary*, vol. 2. Englewood Cliffs, N.J.: Prentice Hall Law & Business, 1993, p. 6.
8. Mary Deibel, "Senate's Spotlight on Ginsburg," *Rocky Mountain News*, July 19, 1993.
9. Bayer, *Ruth Bader Ginsburg*, p. 68.
10. Ibid., p. 77.

CHAPTER 7

1. "Judge Ginsburg Nominated to Replace White on Supreme Court," *Facts on File*, June 17, 1993, p. 443.
2. Margolick, "Trial by Adversity Shapes Jurist's Outlook."
3. Jan Crawford Greenburg, *Supreme Conflict*. New York: The Penguin Press, 2007, p. 171.
4. "Ginsburg Adroit, Amiable but Avoids Specifics," *Congressional Quarterly*, July 24, 1993, p. 1,982.
5. Bayer, *Ruth Bader Ginsburg*, p. 80.
6. "Ginsburg Adroit, Amiable but Avoids Specifics," p. 1,987.

7. Ibid., p. 1,982.
8. Ibid., p. 1,986.
9. U.S. Congress. Senate. *Committee on the Judiciary. Nomination of Ruth Ginsburg to be Associate Justice of the Supreme Court of the United States.* Hearings. 103rd Cong., 1st sess., July 20–23, 1993, p. 139.
10. Ibid., p. 1,988.
11. "Senate Approves Ginsburg for Court," *Rocky Mountain News*, August 4, 1993.

CHAPTER 8

1. Greenburg, *Supreme Conflict*, p. 219.
2. Ibid., p. 220.
3. Toni House and Kathleen Arberg, "And Then There Were Two," *Docket Sheet of the Supreme Court of the United States* 30, no. 1, Fall 1993, p. 3.
4. Ibid.
5. "Winner," *Legal Times*, December 27, 1993, p. 5.
6. Greenburg, *Supreme Conflict*, p. 219.
7. Ibid.
8. Ibid., p. 220.
9. *Almanac of the Federal Judiciary*, vol. 2, p. 7.
10. Bayer, *Ruth Bader Ginsburg*, p. 91.
11. Ibid., p. 95.
12. Ibid., p. 96.
13. Ibid., p. 90.
14. Joan Biskupic, "Supreme Court Invalidates Exclusion of Women by VMI," *Washington Post*, June 27, 1996, p. A1.
15. Sheryl Gay Stolberg, "Ginsburg Leaves Hospital; Prognosis on Cancer Is Good," *New York Times*. September 29, 1999, http://www.nytimes.com/1999/09/29/us/ginsburg-leaves-hospital-prognosis-on-cancer-is-good.html?pagewanted=1.

CHAPTER 9

1. Jeffrey Toobin, *The Nine*. New York: Doubleday, 2007, p. 154.
2. "Ruth Bader Ginsburg and Malvina Harlan," National Public Radio (NPR). May 2, 2002, http://www.npr.org/programs/morning/features/2002/may/ginsburg/.
3. Miriam P. Feinberg and Miriam Klein Shapiro, *Hear Her Voice!* Cedarhurst, N.Y.: Pitspopany Press, 2006, p. 142.

CHAPTER 10

1. Toobin, *The Nine*, p. 248.
2. Ibid, pp. 248–249.
3. Ibid., p. 249.
4. "Conversation Between Justice Ruth Bader Ginsburg & Dean Elena Kagan," *Harvard Journal of Law & Gender*, Summer 2009.
5. Rebecca Traister, "Hell Hath No Fury like Ruth Bader Ginsburg," Salon.com. February 6, 2009, http://www.salon.com/opinion/feature/2009/02/06/ruth_bader_ginsburg/.
6. Ginsburg, J., Dissenting, *Gonzales v. Carhart*. April 18, 2007, http://www.law.cornell.edu/supct/html/05-380.ZD.html.
7. Robert Barnes, "Over Ginsburg's Dissent, Court Limits Bias Suits," *Washington Post*. May 30, 2007, http://www.washingtonpost.com/wp-dyn/content/article/2007/05/29/AR2007052900740.html.
8. "Ruth Bader Ginsburg and Malvina Harlan," NPR.
9. Emily Bazelon, "The Place of Women on the Court," *New York Times*. July 7, 2009, http://www.nytimes.com/2009/07/12/magazine/12ginsburg-t.html?pagewanted=all.

10. Bloomberg News, "Ginsburg Will Have Che-motherapy," *New York Times*. March 18, 2009, http://www.nytimes.com/2009/03/18/us/18brfs-GINSBURGWILL_BRF.html.

11. "Conversation Between Justice Ruth Bader Ginsburg & Dean Elena Kagan."

12. Gardiner Harris, "M.D. Ginsburg, 78, Dies," *New York Times*, June 28, 2010, http://www.nytimes.com/2010/06/28/us/28ginsburg.html

BIBLIOGRAPHY

Ayer, Eleanor H. *Ruth Bader Ginsburg: Fire and Steel on the Supreme Court*. New York: Dillon Press, 1994.

Bayer, Linda. *Ruth Bader Ginsburg*. Philadelphia: Chelsea House Publishers, 2000.

Bredeson, Carmen. *Ruth Bader Ginsburg: Supreme Court Justice*. Springfield, N.J.: Enslow Publishers, Inc., 1995.

Gilbert, Lynn and Gaylen Moore. *Particular Passions: Talks with Women Who Have Shaped Our Times*. New York: Crown Books, 1981.

Swiger, Elinor Porter. *Women Lawyers at Work*. New York: Julian Messner, 1978.

FURTHER RESOURCES

BOOKS

Campbell, Amy Leigh. *Raising the Bar: Ruth Bader Ginsburg and the ACLU Women's Rights Project*. Bloomington, Ind.: Xlibris, 2003.

Feinberg, Miriam P., and Miriam Klein Shapiro. *Hear Her Voice! Twelve Jewish Women Who Changed the World*. Cedarhurst, N.Y.: Pitspopany Press, 2006.

Greenburg, Jan Crawford. *Supreme Conflict: The Inside Story of the Struggle for Control of the United States Supreme Court*. New York: The Penguin Press, 2007.

Jost, Kenneth. *The Supreme Court A to Z, Fourth Edition*. Washington, D.C.: CQ Press, 2007.

Toobin, Jeffrey. *The Nine: Inside the Secret World of the Supreme Court*. New York: Doubleday, 2007.

Tushnet, Mark. *A Court Divided: The Rehnquist Court and the Future of Constitutional Law*. New York: W.W. Norton & Company, 2005.

WEB SITES

The American Civil Liberties Union (ACLU)
http://www.aclu.org/

The Oyez Project
http://www.oyez.org

The Supreme Court of the United States
http://www.supremecourtus.gov/

PICTURE CREDITS

INDEX

Page numbers in *italics* indicate photos or illustrations.

ABOUT THE AUTHOR

PAUL McCAFFREY graduated from the Millbrook School in Millbrook, New York, and received his bachelor's degree from Vassar College in Poughkeepsie, New York. He is currently an editor at the H.W. Wilson Company, a library reference publisher, where he oversees The Reference Shelf series. Among the titles he has edited or co-edited are *The United States Election System* and *The United States Supreme Court*. *Ruth Bader Ginsburg* is his first book for Chelsea House. Raised in Brookfield, Connecticut, he now lives in Brooklyn, New York.

AK